for case you're
serious
Love
mom

7-31-97

"GET ME OUTTA HERE!"

Almost everyone has been there at some point—stuck in a job that is too boring, too low-paying, or simply too dead end. But how can you make a career-change decision that is reasoned, realistic, and achievable? Using charts and a ratings formula, this book gives you the objective tools to examine your career and re-engineer your life—with clear answers to such questions as:

- How long will it take me to find a new job?
- Which industries should I start into?
- What is the best way to prepare for a job interview?
- How risky is starting my own business?
- When should I make the change?

Alternate Selection of **Money**® Book Club™

Starting Over

Money® Magazine

Other books in the
Money ® America's Financial Advisor series:

How to Retire Young and Rich

401(k) Take Charge of Your Future

Paying for Your Child's College Education

The Right Way to Invest in Mutual Funds

Dollar Pinching: A Consumer's Guide to Smart Spending

Car Shopping Made Easy: Buying or Leasing, New or Used

Starting Over

How to Change Careers or Start Your Own Business

Stephen M. Pollan
and Mark Levine

WARNER BOOKS

A Time Warner Company

A NOTE FROM THE PUBLISHER

This publication is designed to provide competent and reliable information regarding the subject matter covered. However, it is sold with the understanding that the author and publisher are not engaged in rendering legal, financial, or other professional advice. Laws and practices often vary from state to state and if legal or other expert assistance is required, the services of a professional should be sought. The author and publisher specifically disclaim any liability that is incurred from the use or application of the contents of this book.

Copyright © 1997 by MONEY magazine
All rights reserved.

Warner Books, Inc., 1271 Avenue of the Americas, New York, NY 10020
Visit our Web site at http://pathfinder.com/twep

W A Time Warner Company

Printed in the United States of America
First Printing: March 1997
10 9 8 7 6 5 4 3 2 1

Library of Congress Cataloging-in-Publication Data

Pollan, Stephen M.
    Starting over : how to change careers or start your own business /
Stephen M. Pollan and Mark Levine.
        p. cm.
    Includes index.
    ISBN 0-446-67166-5
    1. Career changes. 2. Job hunting. 3. Self-employed. 4. New
business enterprises—Management. I. Levine, Mark, 1958–
II. Title.
HF5384.P65   1997
650.1—dc20   96-21475
                                                                  CIP

Book design and composition by L&G McRee
Cover design by Bernadette Evangelist
Cover illustration by Peter Hoey

To every person who says "I hate my job" and has the guts, determination, and prudence to do something rational about it.

ACKNOWLEDGMENTS

The authors would like to thank Richard Eisenberg and Rick Wolff for their advice, Stuart Krichevsky and Jane Morrow for their guidance, and Corky Pollan and Deirdre Martin Levine for their unflinching support.

CONTENTS

Starting Over

CHAPTER 1

Shock Treatment

It's obvious there are monumental changes rocking the workplace today. Nearly every magazine writer, every academic, every manager, and even every politician is telling us all about the "workplace revolution" that's taking place.

You've heard "corporate paternalism" is dead and how glad we should be about its demise: we'll now be able to spread our wings and not be inhibited by that overbearing "parent."

You've read we're no longer limited to climbing one specific corporate ladder and that we'll switch jobs—maybe even industries or careers—three, or five, or seven different times during our lives.

And it's likely you've seen all the books, by academics and career experts, seeking to define this workplace revolution with a catchy name and an insightful philosophy guaranteed to go over well on *Oprah*.

I'm sure none of this comes as a shock to you. You'd have to be deaf, dumb, and blind not to have realized the job market has changed. But what's shocking, at least to me, is that nobody is focusing on the nuts and bolts of this revolution.

I've seen hundreds of articles and almost as many books discussing the reasons why the workplace has changed and what the job market will look like in the year 2050. Optimists talk of a nation of entrepreneurs living in pastoral cabins, commuting to work by modems and fax machines. Pessimists write of the end of work as we know it and predict class warfare unless we enact equally dramatic shifts in public policy. But nobody is writing about how the 45-year-old product manager for Acme Inc. deals with this revolution.

Sure, it's fascinating to read about the future and debate the sociological ramifications of what's going on in the workplace. It can be equally interesting to sit down with a career counselor and, through fantasizing and role-playing, come up with a description of your dream job. But neither helps you if you're sitting at your desk worrying about when the ax will fall, knowing that when (not if) it does, you're going to have an incredibly tough time finding another job. And even if you do find a job, it's probably going to pay a lot less and not offer anywhere near the same kinds of benefits you're getting now.

I've written this book to fill that void.

Let me say right up front: I'm not a career counselor. And I'm certainly not an expert on the sociology of the workplace. What I do is help people solve their problems. For more than three decades I've been offering advice, guidance, and empowerment to clients as an attorney and financial consultant. I help people buy and sell homes, start businesses, plan home renovations, negotiate contracts, and, for the past few years, deal with career crises.

I've helped clients negotiate employment contracts and severance deals. I've helped clients quit when they were forced to, get new jobs when they had to, and start businesses when they wanted to.

At least once a week for the past two years someone calls my office to make an appointment, saying, "I hate my job. . . . I want to speak to Stephen about what I should do." And I help them decide.

Don't get me wrong. I don't have a miracle cure for job dissatisfaction. And I'm not qualified to dig into your psyche and help you come to terms with your deep-seated desire to be a juggler. What I have is an approach. I sit down with a client and together we figure out what's upsetting him, what his options are, what the best solution is, and how he should go about enacting it.

Clients come to me for quick results, for solutions to their problems. They're looking for shock treatments, not long-term therapy or preventive medicine. That's what I provide them with—and what I'll provide you with in the rest of this book.

If you're looking to find out what your dream job is, or what you'd be perfect doing, you've picked up the wrong book. But if you're in pain and want that pain to stop, *now*, you're in the right place. Rather than focusing on you and your emotions, I focus on your job and your pragmatic options.

I'm well aware of the potential benefits of long-term counseling and getting in touch with your inner feelings about your career. I've the utmost respect for career counselors. But in these frenetic and dangerous times long-term solutions simply take too long to accomplish. Halfway through your career counseling, while you're still trying to determine whether you're a "motivator" or a "builder," you're apt to be fired or laid off.

If traditional career counseling is like traditional psychotherapy, my approach is like cognitive therapy: together, you and I will focus on one problem and try to solve it. And in this case, the problem is your job.

CHAPTER 2

You're Not Alone

Since you've picked up this book and have gotten this far into it, it's obvious you're not happy at your job and you're looking to make a change. It's also obvious you want that change to take place sooner rather than later; otherwise you'd have put this book down and started figuring out the color of your parachute. Before we get into the specifics about what's upsetting you, it's important you realize you're not alone in feeling this way and that it's through no fault of your own.

You're probably aware there are others at your place of business who feel just as miserable about their jobs as you do. Maybe you've heard whispered complaints in the lunch room, or a few of you have actually spilled your guts over a piña colada after work. Anyway, since the most recent round of layoffs in your firm, anyone who isn't angry and anxious either owns the company or is Forrest Gump.

You may even know of other companies in your industry where people are just as miserable. Perhaps you and some friendly competitors let down your hair at a recent trade show. Or maybe you've read the headlines in the trade press about layoffs all over the industry.

But what you may not know is that most Americans—not just those in your company or industry—are just as upset and angry and worried about their jobs as you and your peers.

- According to a recent article in *Utne Reader*, 64% of Americans between the ages of 25 and 49 fantasize about quitting their jobs to live on a desert island, travel around the world, or escape the rat race in one way or another.
- One of Yankelovich Partners' most recent surveys of attitudes showed that Americans are disaffected from work and have stopped believing in employer loyalty or the value of experience.
- According to another poll by Yankelovich Partners, 66% of Americans believe job security has deteriorated, and 53% think this insecurity will be long-term.
- In a poll the Gallup Organization conducted for the National Career Development Association, barely 50% of respondents said they like their job enough that they didn't want to leave it.

And it's not just middle- and working-class people who feel this way. According to an article in *Management Review*, one networking group of Connecticut executives who earn more than $100,000 reports 60% of its members think *they'll* lose their jobs in the coming year.

This Isn't Your Average, Everyday Complaining

Sure, people have always griped about their jobs. One of the easiest ways to make a connection with someone new has always been to bitch about your bosses. You're at a party standing next to someone you've just met. First you talk about the weather. Then you talk about your kids and your wife. Next you talk about what a wonderful party it is and what nice folks the hosts are. Finally you start complaining about your job.

What's going on today isn't just run-of-the-mill grumbling. And what you're feeling isn't traditional job-related anxiety. It's a whole new ball game out there—one that the average working American is losing.

Four new factors are contributing to your fears and anger about your job, which, in tandem with an underlying problem that has always been there, are leading to this wholesale disaffection from work.

Technology Is Eliminating or Changing Your Job

There isn't yet enough evidence to resolve the debate over whether information technology—such as the personal computer—destroys more jobs than it creates or vice versa. My guess is that in the long run this new technology, like all previous new technologies, will end up creating more jobs than it destroys. However, that's in the long run. In the here and now, technology is costing jobs.

• According to William Bridges, author of *Job Shift: How to Prosper in a Workplace without Jobs* (Addison-Wesley, 1994), the ratio of permanently terminated workers to temporarily laid off workers was 1.5 to 1 in 1975. In 1982, during the depths of the recession, it was 2 to 1. Today, during what's supposed to be an economic recovery, it's 4 to 1.

Some jobs are clearly being eliminated by technology. Today, one woman sitting at a computer can control a group of robots that can do the jobs of 10 women. Or another woman, sitting at a computer, can do the bookkeeping and billing previously done by an office of six women. In my small five-person office, for instance, the part-time bookkeeper has been replaced by a software program.

Other jobs are being changed by technology. Middle managers used to receive orders from up high and pass them on to their staff. Today lots of middle managers don't have a staff anymore. Rather than delegating, they're doing. The public relations manager is producing her own brochures and mailings using desktop publishing software and a color laser printer. The sales manager is creating her own presentations, making her own travel plans, and managing her own contacts, all with her laptop computer. In my office, the office manager is doing the books and paying the bills herself, rather than delegating the task to a bookkeeper.

Technology today has the power to both change and eliminate your job. And while the former may be empowering to some, the latter is dangerous and frightening to all. Sure, a portion of middle managers are thrilled at being able to do everything themselves (regardless of how many more hours they're now working). But according to the American Management Association, it's these very middle managers who, while making up only 5% to 8% of the workforce, have made up 17% of layoffs.

The Employer/Employee Contract Has Been Torn Up

While few American workers actually had formal contracts, almost everyone works under an implied agreement. The terms of it used to be as follows:

- Show up on time and do what you're told and you'll never be fired.
- Every year you're on the job you'll get an incremental raise.
- Stay late and do your job well and you'll be promoted and maybe even get a bigger raise.
- Stick around until you're 65 and you'll get a pension and a Rolex.

Today you've a better chance of getting a Rolex from a street vendor than from a corporation. That implied contract you worked under for years has been torn into tens of millions of pink slips and severance checks.

All sorts of villains are being blamed for this: the recession of the 1980s, Ronald Reagan, economic globalization and deregulation leading to increased competition, Bill Clinton, NAFTA, Bill Gates, and technology eliminating the need for layers of staff. Whatever or whomever you choose to blame doesn't really matter. What matters is the result. There's a new contract, and the following seem to be its terms:

- You're expendable no matter how long you've been here or how clean you've kept your nose.
- We'll fire you if we need to no matter how good you are at what you do.
- You're lucky to have a job, so forget about a raise.
- There's no corporate ladder, so forget about getting a promotion.
- You'll be lucky to last five years (anyway, we don't offer pensions anymore).
- And while we're at it, we also need you to be more innovative, risk taking, and committed to our goals.

Working under this kind of contract, informal or not, it's no wonder most Americans are miserable and would love to start over if they only could.

The Jobs Being Created Are Worse Than the Jobs Being Destroyed

There's no question the American economy is creating jobs. The problem is the kinds of jobs it's creating. Rather than executive positions at Pepsico's corporate headquarters, they're fry cook jobs at its Taco Bell restaurants. Instead of middle-manager spots at Eastman Kodak in Rochester, they're openings for minilab managers in Podunk. It's Wal-Mart rather than GM that's doing the hiring. And all too often the new jobs are part-time positions with little or no benefits. According to the Bureau of Labor Statistics:

- Of the 18 million jobs created between 1983 and 1993, 20% were part-time or temporary positions.
- Never have so many of the nation's part-time workers wanted to be full-time workers.
- The number of people working for temporary agencies has increased around 240% in the past decade.
- The number of agencies offering temporary professionals and executives has almost tripled in the past four years.
- Today the nation's largest private employer isn't General Motors (400,000) or IBM (255,000), it's Manpower, a temporary employment agency (600,000).

According to some experts, one out of every four American workers is now a "contingency worker"—either a part-timer, a freelancer, an independent contractor, a temp, or an independent professional.

The pundits and would-be politicians are looking for someone to blame for this downgrading of the status, pay, and benefits of new positions and are targeting political incumbents, foreigners, and all the other usual suspects. Actually there's a simple explanation for what's going on.

A century ago our nation (and much of the world) made the shift from an agricultural to an industrial economy. In the process people left the country and came to the city, and the status, pay, and benefits of jobs were upgraded.

Now our nation (and much of the world) is making the shift from an industrial to a service economy. Industrial economies employ lots of relatively well paid production workers. Service economies employ large numbers of lower-paid workers. Why? Well, for one thing, unions never made the inroads into service jobs they did into industrial positions.

Career Is Now Forever

It used to be easier to deal with, or at least accept, job dissatisfaction. All you had to do was put in your time until you qualified for your pension, and then you could tell the boss to take his job and shove it. Now, not only are you unlikely to get anywhere near as lucrative a pension (if any) from your boss, but you can't rely on Social Security being around to supplement your savings and investments. If you're a baby boomer, you're also facing potentially huge college tuition and elder care bills.

All this adds up to your not being able to retire, whether you want to or not. You're going to need an earned income for a lot longer than your parents did. For those who like what they're doing, that's great. They can just keep on enjoying themselves until they drop. But for those who hate their jobs, this just means the one hope for salvation—retirement—is gone.

Add increased longevity to the mix and it's not a pretty picture: not only could you be working a job you hate until you drop, but you might not be dropping until 80 or 90.

You Got Into This Career by Default . . . or When You Were a Different Person

Finally, there's an underlying problem contributing to the job malaise, one that we're just now starting to focus on. Most of us got into our current job or career by default rather than design.

- In a poll the Gallup Organization conducted for the National Career Development Association, only 36% of Americans said they started their present jobs or careers because they made a conscious choice or followed a definite plan.
- In the same poll, 72% of respondents said if they could start over, they'd get more information about their career options.

Perhaps our folks or a teacher pushed us in a direction—that's why I became a lawyer. Maybe we just took the first job we were offered in the field we studied—that's how my coauthor got into magazine publishing. Once in an industry or on a career path, we just stayed there, partly because it made economic sense (it would be tough getting the same money elsewhere) and partly because it was just the way we did things.

Even if you were one of the few who made a conscious choice about where you'd get a job, you're apt to be unhappy. Since that day you entered a field by design, not only has the field and the job market changed, but so have you. You've matured. Your interests have changed. Your values have evolved. You've got mouths to feed and a mortgage to pay. But you're still in the same field.

None of This Is Your Fault

Not only do I want you to come away from this chapter knowing you're not alone in feeling unhappy at work, but I also want you to realize none of this is your fault.

Let's look at those five factors once again.

TECHNOLOGY IS ELIMINATING OR CHANGING YOUR JOB

Unless you're the guy who invented the microchip, you had nothing to do with this. Not only that, but there's no way you or I or anyone is going to stop the technological locomotive. The Luddites couldn't stop weaving machines, and no modern-day technophobe is going to slow down information technology.

THE EMPLOYER/EMPLOYEE CONTRACT HAS BEEN TORN UP

Unless you're the fellow who coined today's most popular euphemism, downsizing, you had nothing to do with this, either. Not only that, but the only thing you can do about it is "get with the program."

THE JOBS BEING CREATED ARE WORSE
THAN THE JOBS BEING DESTROYED

Yet again, this is just a fact of economic life. And unless you're going to go out and devote your life to the organizing of service industry workers, there's little you can do about it.

CAREER IS NOW FOREVER

Okay, by taking care of yourself you *are* partly responsible for increased longevity. But what's the alternative? Take up smoking so you die rather than work at the bank for another 20 years? You and all your fellow baby boomers could bankrupt your kids by insisting on keeping Social Security afloat, but I don't think that's likely to happen, either.

YOU GOT INTO THIS CAREER BY DEFAULT . . .
OR WHEN YOU WERE A DIFFERENT PERSON

What did you know? You were just a kid. And you can't even blame your folks too much. They were just doing what they thought was best for you. And you sure can't turn back the clock and do things over now . . . or can you?

Take Charge of Your Future

You can't change the past. And you can't stop the societal and economic forces impacting your life. But you *can* change the way you respond to them. Rather than being resigned to your fate, you can take charge of your future. You may not be able to change the cards you've been dealt, but you can play your hand to the best of your abilities.

That's what the rest of this book will help you do: start over in a way that's feasible and practical. This isn't a book of dreams and fantasies; it's a book of pragmatic solutions to real problems. My goal is to enable you to actually start over, not just dream about it. And I'm not going to rely on empowering language. I'm going to offer realistic strategies and plans. But before I can set you on the right course I've got to get you to turn your abstract laments into concrete complaints. That's what we'll do in Chapter 3.

For More Information

For more sources of information about the changes taking place in the job market and the American economy, take a look at Appendix One on page 199.

CHAPTER 3

Getting Specific

Whenever a new client calls my office I try to get an idea of his problem before his appointment. That way I can prepare for the meeting so it's a working session rather than just an introductory session. In most instances it's pretty simple. Either I or one of my office staff asks, "What's wrong?" or, "What do you need help with?" But when the client's calling for a job or career consultation, finding out what's wrong is a bit more complicated.

"I hate my job—it's killing me" is probably the most common response, followed closely by things like

- "I feel as if I'm in prison."
- "I'm being taken advantage of."
- "I just can't get out of bed."
- "It's just not enough anymore."
- "I'm not going anywhere."
- "I'm wasting my life."

When I or my staff hear one of these or a similar explanation, I know that the goal of my first meeting is to get him to devel-

17

op a list of specific complaints about his job. That's also the goal of this chapter.

Jobs Are Catch-alls for Unhappiness

For better or worse, many of us tie our identities as individuals very tightly to our occupations. We see ourselves and present ourselves to others by explaining what it is we do for a living. Think about it. When you meet someone for the first time, what's one of the first questions you ask or are asked? I'll bet it's "What do you do?" That question could be answered a million different ways, since we all "do" a million different things. But the anticipated answer is to explain what you do to earn money.

Once you've mentioned your occupation, and have learned of the other person's occupation, there's a millisecond of delay. Consciously or unconsciously the two of you are sizing each other up, trying to establish who's more powerful, who makes more money, who has greater status, maybe even who's more intelligent. Job is so central to our notion of identity, we assume knowing what a person does for a living tells us almost everything there is to know about him—or at least enough for us to compare ourselves to him.

First of all, such assumptions are factually wrong. I have clients who are national media personalities who make less money than other clients of mine who are carpenters and plumbers. I have some retailer clients who are far more intelligent than some of my college professor clients. I work closely with people in hundreds of different professions, and I can attest to the fact that you cannot judge a person by his occupation.

But while such an attitude is dead wrong, it does show how our jobs become the catch-alls for our feelings about ourselves and our lives. Our careers are convenient whipping boys for everything that's going wrong in our personal lives. Had a fight with your wife? Blame your boss for putting you in a bad mood. Your son upset with you? Blame your job for not letting you spend time with him. Neighbor complains about your yard? It's your job's fault for taking time away from your mowing.

Simply put, it's easier to blame our boss or our job than ourselves or anyone else we're close to, for that matter. It's certainly a lot less painful. And it also lets us shrug off the situation by saying that since our job is at fault, there's nothing we can really do about it. After all, they call it work, not fun. So someone keeps shrugging things off until they build to an intolerable level, and then he explodes, calls my office, and says his job is killing him.

Getting Specific Gets Rid of the Emotions and Makes Problems Solvable

Obviously, unless you're being exposed to nuclear radiation or asbestos on a daily basis at work, your job really isn't killing you. You may have problems with your job, but it's probably not that you're being killed by it.

I know I'm being a bit flippant, but I'm trying to make a point. When you define problems in abstract, emotional, and general terms, the only way they can be dealt with is philosophically. When you define problems in specific, rational, and concrete terms, they can be dealt with pragmatically. If you say "I hate my job," I can't help you. But if you say "The environment at work is too stressful," I can.

This isn't just a matter of semantics, it's perception as well. By forcing you to give specific reasons for not being happy at work, I'm helping you clear away all the emotions clouding the real workplace issues. Once we get your real problems in sharp focus, we can address them.

The Eight Primary Job Problems

If you were coming into my office for a personal consultation, I could work with you in coming up with your own list of specific problems. But since this is a book and I can't work with each reader one on one, I'm going to have to take a shortcut.

After more than three decades of consulting with people about their financial lives, I've come up with a list of eight primary problems people have with their jobs.

And just as it was essential for you to transform a general feeling of unhappiness into specific problems for us to come up with solutions, so too do you have to pick the problem(s) that are most pressing. So from this list, select the one or two problems you most identify with.

MY JOB IS TOO STRESSFUL

The key here is to make sure the stress is coming from your job, not from something else. If you're the type of guy who gets stressed out selecting socks, then it's probably not your job at the library that's giving you the shakes. But if you're the type who can doze off on a roller coaster, but you've been unable to sleep since you became a patrolman for the Sarajevo Police Department, then it's safe to assume your job is the cause.

MY JOB IS TOO TIME-CONSUMING

The 40-hour work week has gone the way of carbon paper. However, if your baby keeps crying when you pick him up, but stops when your baby-sitter picks him up, or if your 10-year-old is more concerned about having Grandpa come to his baseball game than you, I think you're putting in too much time at work.

MY JOB ISN'T FINANCIALLY REWARDING

Everyone wishes he earned more money. But if your meager salary is standing in the way of things you and your family need, rather than just want, than clearly you're in need of more bucks.

MY JOB ISN'T EMOTIONALLY/PSYCHOLOGICALLY/ SPIRITUALLY REWARDING

A Wall Street investment banker can contribute just as much to the betterment of the world as someone who's teaching blind Native American orphans. If *you* truly find your work unrewarding, then let's deal with the problem. If you're afraid others think your work isn't meaningful and that's why you're unhappy, the problem is with you, not your job.

THERE'S NO PLACE FOR ME TO MOVE UP, FINANCIALLY OR OTHERWISE, IN MY COMPANY

Rather than climbing a ladder that your employer sets in front of you, the path to advancement today is like hacking your own path through a jungle—not only do you have to do it yourself, but there's no telling in which direction you'll have to turn in order to keep progressing. I believe that feeling your growth within a company is blocked is always a valid reason to start over.

THERE'S NO PLACE FOR ME TO MOVE UP, FINANCIALLY OR OTHERWISE, IN MY INDUSTRY

This problem isn't as common as being blocked inside a company. That's good, because it's a far more difficult problem to solve. If this is one of your problems, it's definitely a reason to start over.

MY JOB IS NO LONGER CHALLENGING

If you're one of those restless souls always looking for new challenges, be forewarned: you're probably never going to be satisfied. If you use this restlessness as the sole rationale for starting over, you'll never spend more than a year in any one spot. But if you have the potential to be satisfied, and you're not, there's definitely something wrong. It's time to start over.

MY WORKPLACE IS AN UNHEALTHY ENVIRONMENT

There's no reason for you to work a job that makes you physically or mentally ill. Don't be a martyr. And take heart—this is the easiest of the problems to solve.

Now that we've narrowed down your free-floating unhappiness about your job to one or two specific complaints, we can turn to the other side of the equation.

There's a common piece of advice that's always offered to people looking to start over, one I'm sure you've heard many times in your life: The world is your oyster—your choices are limitless. The problem with this piece of advice is it's dead wrong. Your choices aren't limitless. You've only got nine.

The Nine Options

Whenever I tell a client that he doesn't have unlimited choices he gets angry with me. "What do you mean there are only nine things I can do?" he snaps. "I can do anything I want." You're probably reacting the same way. But before you throw down this book in a fit of rage, give me a chance to explain.

You're absolutely right in that you can do anything you want. You can run away and join the circus. You can open a store selling chocolate-covered bagels. You can give up your job at the IRS and try out for quarterback of the Dallas Cowboys. However, if you want to actually *do* something as opposed to just *talk* about doing something, you need to look at your options in a different way. Rather than being overwhelmed with the millions of paths you could pursue, my suggestion is to focus instead on the process of starting over.

For instance, let's look at Dick Salem, an accountant, working in the finance department of an automotive manufacturer.

Let's say Dick decides to look for a job in the finance department of another automotive manufacturer. He'd be *getting another job in the same career and industry*.

If he chose to look for another accounting job, but in the aerospace industry, he'd be *getting another job in the same career but a different industry*.

If Dick decided he wanted to stay in the automotive industry, but as a marketing person instead, he'd be *getting another job in the same industry but a different career.*

If he suddenly decided to pursue his lifelong fantasy of becoming quarterback for the Green Bay Packers, Dick would be *getting another job in a different career in a different industry.*

If Dick decided to open his own business, offering financial services to the automotive industry, he'd be *starting a business in the same industry.*

If instead he wanted to open his own store selling chocolate-covered bagels, he'd be *starting a business in a different industry.*

If Dick opted to leave National Motors and go back to school to get his degree in retail management, while working in a bookstore, he'd be *going back to school and getting a part-time job.*

If suddenly Dick decided to quit his job, sell most of his possessions, and get a job repairing bicycles in a small town in upstate New York, he'd be placing less emphasis on his job and more on his personal life or, to use the current term, *downshifting.*

And if, after exploring all his other options, Dick decides his job at National Motors isn't that bad after all, he'd be *staying where he is.*

Framing your options in this matter makes it much easier to see exactly what such shifts would, might, or wouldn't do for you. And that makes it much easier to pick a direction and actually pursue it. All it takes is six steps.

CHAPTER 4

Weighing Your Options and Choosing One

At first glance, reducing your options from an infinite number to nine makes the process of choosing one a lot easier. But all we've really done is take something that was impossible and make it possible. In order to make the starting over process truly doable, we've got to go further. I suggest following a logical six-step process.

Step 1: Outline the Advantages and Disadvantages of the Option or Options You Find Attractive.

List all of the potential advantages to making this kind of a move. Feel free to be as optimistic as you want. Of course, you also need to list all the potential disadvantages. In coming up with your answers, you should be as pessimistic as you were optimistic in coming up with the list of advantages. I've come up with some general advantages and disadvantages of each option. Use these as starting points for your own customized lists.

GET ANOTHER JOB IN THE SAME CAREER IN THE SAME INDUSTRY

Advantages

- Can get you out of an ugly situation
- Can get you into a new location
- Relatively easy if you're in a growing industry or a career that's in demand
- You won't have to prove anything to anyone
- Provides a chance to turn over a new leaf
- Provides a chance to increase your salary substantially
- Provides a chance to negotiate "quality of life" benefits, such as flextime and telecommuting
- They really want you to come on board—not only do they get the benefit of your services, but they're depriving a competitor of your services

Disadvantages

- Tough to do if your industry is in a slump or your career isn't in demand
- Won't add new skills to your résumé
- Really a superficial rather than substantive change
- You might have to relocate
- You might have to adjust to a new corporate culture
- The new environment may end up being no better than the old environment
- Reinforces your linkage to a specific industry

GET ANOTHER JOB IN THE SAME CAREER BUT A DIFFERENT INDUSTRY

Advantages

- Adds flexibility to the list of skills on your résumé
- Could increase your salary
- Could inspire you, revitalizing your feelings about your career
- May provide more chances for advancement
- Could provide more relative security, if you're moving to a more stable industry
- Provides a chance to shine since you can bring a fresh approach to problems
- Provides a chance to turn over a new leaf
- Can get you out of an ugly situation
- Can get you into a new location

Disadvantages

- Such a nontraditional move could be threatening to your new co-workers
- You'll have to prove your skills and their applicability
- You'll have some learning to do in order to excel
- You'll definitely have to deal with a new corporate culture
- You'll have to develop new aspects of your skill
- You might be moving to a less secure, less stable industry
- You may have to accept less money than you're making now
- You might have to relocate
- The new environment may end up being no better than the old environment

GET ANOTHER JOB IN THE SAME INDUSTRY BUT A DIFFERENT CAREER

Advantages

- You already know all the players
- Will be easier to prove your skills are transferable
- Could be challenging and exciting
- Not as unconventional as it once was
- Could mean an increase in salary
- Could offer more opportunities to advance
- Allows you to expand the skill list on your résumé
- Adds flexibility to the skill list on your résumé
- Could move you to a better environment

Disadvantages

- Requires a substantial step backward in terms of seniority and maybe status
- While higher-ups may no longer see it as unconventional, peers will still perceive you as a threat
- Could require a substantial cut in salary
- Since you've no track record you'll have to prove yourself
- Reinforces your linkage to a particular industry
- The new environment may end up being no better than the old environment

GET ANOTHER JOB IN A DIFFERENT INDUSTRY AND A DIFFERENT CAREER

Advantages

- Conceivably this could satisfy all your needs and wants
- You'll be able to turn over a new leaf

Disadvantages

- It's likely that you'll fail since you've no experience
- Could be viewed as a capricious move
- Almost certainly will result in a significant decrease in salary
- The older you are, the tougher this will be to do
- Once you've made such a move there's no way you'll ever be able to come back
- This is so unconventional, superiors will certainly view you with suspicion and peers will definitely see you as a threat
- Likely to require you to relocate
- Requires a tremendous investment in time to climb back to the level you left

START YOUR OWN BUSINESS IN THE SAME INDUSTRY

Advantages

- Offers you freedom and total control over your work life
- Provides a chance to relocate
- Provides a chance to improve your quality of life
- Provides a chance to use your creativity
- Expands the list of skills on your résumé
- Provides a chance to increase your income

- You can take advantage of your reputation
- You know all the players
- Your skills are entirely transferable

Disadvantages

- Offers less status
- Your lifestyle may suffer
- There will be no boundaries between your work and personal life
- Inherently risky financially
- You'll have to work longer hours
- Your income may suffer, and your savings and/or credit certainly will
- You'll be responsible for structuring your own life

START YOUR OWN BUSINESS IN A DIFFERENT INDUSTRY

Advantages

- Offers you freedom and total control over your work life
- Provides a chance to relocate
- Provides a chance to improve your quality of life
- Provides a chance to use your creativity
- Expands the list of skills on your résumé
- Provides a chance to increase your income

Disadvantages

- You can't take advantage of your reputation
- You don't know all the players
- Your skills aren't transferable

- Offers less status
- Your lifestyle may suffer
- There will be no boundaries between your work and personal life
- Inherently risky financially
- You'll have to work longer hours
- Your income may suffer, and your savings and/or credit certainly will
- You'll be responsible for structuring your own life

GO BACK TO SCHOOL AND GET A PART-TIME JOB

Advantages

- You can truly start your career over, but this time with lots of real-world skills and maturity
- If it's an interim step to any of the other options, it decreases their risk and increases their feasibility by a factor of two

Disadvantages

- Means a tremendous financial sacrifice in both income and savings or credit
- Means an extraordinary drop in status
- Means a tremendous lifestyle sacrifice
- Means a tremendous time sacrifice
- Can be difficult to adjust to academic environment
- Nearly everyone you know will focus on the roadblocks

DOWNSHIFT (PLACE LESS EMPHASIS ON YOUR JOB AND MORE ON YOUR PERSONAL LIFE)

Advantages

- Places the emphasis on spiritual, psychological, and emotional rewards, not on money
- Offers you time to spend doing what you love or care about
- Potentially offers less stress, if you accept the disadvantages

Disadvantages

- Means a dramatic reduction in income
- Means a dramatic reduction in status
- Means a dramatic reduction in lifestyle
- Means a dramatic reduction in mobility
- Once you "downshift" it will be extraordinarily difficult to reenter the regular workplace

STAY WHERE YOU ARE

Advantages

- You can approach your job with a new perspective
- There are no risks
- There are no surprises
- All the advantages your current job offers

Disadvantages

- It still requires some time and effort
- All the disadvantages your current job offers

Step 2: Determine Which Options Will Solve Your Primary Problem(s).

This is perhaps the most important step in your analysis of the options you're considering. After all, you've already pinpointed your one or two major problems with your current job or career. Why go through all the effort required if it's not going to solve your problem? And as you can see from the chart on page 34, not every option solves every problem.

Focus on the one or two major problems you have with your current job. It's pretty obvious that if you want to solve your problem, you should pick an option that will, in fact, solve it.

I chose the word "will" intentionally. I don't think you should choose a course that only "could" solve your primary problem. If you're going to go through all the time and effort involved in truly starting over, you should have a guarantee that your pain will be eliminated.

Find the row in the chart on page 34 that represents your number one problem. Scan across the row, noting which of the nine options *will* solve your problem. Those are the only options you should even consider.

Do the same for your number two problem. See if there are any options that *will* solve both your number one and number two problems. If there are none, see if there are any options that *will* solve your number one problem and *could* solve your number two problem. If you can't come up with any option that fits that description, throw out your number two problem. Simply accept you can't solve both problems and it's more important to solve your primary complaint.

To compare options to one another you need to look at how feasible each is, how much risk each entails, and how much time each would need.

33

Symbols

√ means the option *will* solve the problem

? means the option *could* solve the problem

X means the option *won't* solve the problem

Problems

• Problem 1: My job is too stressful.

• Problem 2: My job is too time-consuming.

• Problem 3: My job isn't financially rewarding.

• Problem 4: My job isn't emotionally/psychologically/spiritually rewarding.

• Problem 5: There's no place for me to move up in my company.

• Problem 6: There's no place for me to move up in my industry.

• Problem 7: My job is no longer challenging.

• Problem 8: My workplace is an unhealthy environment.

Options

• Option 1: Get another job in the same career in the same industry

• Option 2: Get another job in the same career but in a different industry

• Option 3: Get another job in the same industry but in a different career

• Option 4: Get another job in a different industry and a different career

• Option 5: Start your own business in the same industry

• Option 6: Start your own business in a different industry

• Option 7: Go back to school and get a part-time job

• Option 8: Downshift

• Option 9: Stay where you are

	Opt 1	Opt 2	Opt 3	Opt 4	Opt 5	Opt 6	Opt 7	Opt 8	Opt 9
Prob 1	X	X	?	?	X	X	√	√	X
Prob 2	X	X	X	?	X	X	√	√	X
Prob 3	√	?	?	?	√	?	X	X	X
Prob 4	?	?	√	?	√	√	√	√	X
Prob 5	√	√	√	√	√	√	√	X	X
Prob 6	X	√	X	√	√	√	√	X	X
Prob 7	?	?	√	√	√	√	√	X	X
Prob 8	√	√	√	√	√	√	√	√	X

Step 3: Analyze the Feasibility and Risk of Each Option and How Much Time Each Requires.

FEASIBILITY

How easy is it to make such a move? For instance, if you're the only person who has to take action or make a decision, it's a cinch. If you need to get someone else to go along with you, that makes it a bit tougher.

In order to make comparison possible, I've scored the feasibility of each option on a scale of from one to five.

- A feasibility score of one means you can do it in your sleep.
- A feasibility score of two means it takes more effort than breathing . . . but not much.
- A feasibility score of three means it's doable, but you'll have to work up a sweat.
- A feasibility score of four means it's tough work with no guarantee of success.
- A feasibility score of five means it's just about impossible no matter how hard you try.

RISK

There's no such thing as a risk-free life. You could get hit by lightning when you're out raking leaves. But some actions are, by their very nature, riskier than others. Once again, in order to make comparison easier I've scored each option on a risk scale of from one to five.

- A risk factor of one means it's as dangerous as taking a nap.
- A risk factor of two means it's as dangerous as walking across the street—just look both ways.
- A risk factor of three means it's as dangerous as driving a car—you've got to pay attention.
- A risk factor of four means it's as dangerous as driving your car in an ice storm—sure, you could make it, but you're taking your life in your hands.
- A risk factor of five means it's as dangerous as jumping out of a plane without a parachute—yes, some who have done it have survived, but not many.

TIMING

Almost every one of these options takes time. And that's time spent either by staying in a job you hate or by putting the pieces and money in place to make the move. I've made some time estimates for each. I've tried to be both conservative and realistic. In order to make comparison easier I've expressed each in terms of months. I've also sometimes suggested tips for speeding up the process.

Take a look at the chart on page 37. Look in the left column for the options that you've determined will solve your primary problem and either will or could solve your secondary problem.

First, compare their feasibility factors. Which of the options that solve your problem is the most feasible?

Second, compare their risk factors. Which of the options that solve your problem is the safest?

Finally, compare the amount of time it will take to accomplish each. Which of the options that solve your problem can be accomplished quickest?

	Feasibility	Risk	Time (months)
Get another job in the same career in the same industry	Growing biz: 2 Shrinking biz: 4	2	1 per $10K
Get another job in the same career but in a different industry	4	Growing biz: 2 Shrinking biz: 4	6 plus 1 per $10K
Get another job in the same industry but in a different career	Staid biz: 4 Creative biz: 3	3.5	12 plus 1 per $10K
Get another job in a different industry and a different career	5+	5	Entry level: 6 Near same $: 24 plus 1 per $10K
Start your own business in the same industry	1	Original: 5 Franchise or preexisting: 5	Original: 9 to 12 Franchise or preexisting: 6 to 9
Start your own business in a different industry	1	Original: 5+ Franchise or preexisting: 5	Original: 9 to 12 Franchise or preexisting: 6 to 9
Go back to school and get a part-time job	2	2	Depends on savings and spousal income
Downshift	1	1	12
Stay where you are	1	1	0

Some Interesting Observations

Before you move on to the next step, let's take a couple of moments to examine the charts on pages 34 and 37. By looking at work-related problems and possible solutions in this graphic manner, we're able to make some interesting observations, observations that can not only clarify your current situation, but can help to put into perspective your lifelong relationship to work.

- The option that's the most feasible, the least risky, and the quickest to accomplish is the one that solves the fewest problems: staying where you are.
- The next safest and easiest to accomplish options are the ones that offer you no chances of increasing your income: downshifting and going back to school.
- Entrepreneurial options are both highly risky and very feasible.
- Making a radical shift while staying in the job market (getting another job in a different career and different industry) is simultaneously very risky, hard to do, and extremely time-consuming.
- The most common choices—getting another job in the same career in the same industry, getting another job in the same career but a different industry, and getting another job in the same industry but a different career—are all similar in their feasibility and risk. The main difference among them seems to be how long they take to accomplish.
- The most difficult problems to solve are feeling stressed out and feeling as if you don't have enough time.
- Feeling as though you're not reaping sufficient financial rewards is just as tough to *definitely* solve but offers a lot more *potential* solutions.
- The easiest problem to solve is an unhealthy environment. The only option that won't solve it is staying put.
- The next easiest problem to solve is having nowhere to go in

your company. Any option that gets you out of the company, but keeps you gainfully employed, solves it.

• Aside from staying put, the options that solve the fewest problems are the two most common: getting another job in the same career in the same industry, and getting another job in the same career but in a different industry.

• The option that solves the most problems is the one that's pursued the least often: going back to school and getting a part-time job.

• The next most powerful option is starting your own business in the same industry you're currently working in.

Now that I've given you some food for future career thought, let's get back to your current situation. The next two steps in the process focus on determining how much of a financial cushion you need to start over, and coming up with the money.

Step 4: Analyze Whether Your Present Resources Are Sufficient to Support You While You're Starting Over.

Everyone who hates his current job would love to be able to quit tomorrow and launch his program to start over. Unfortunately that's impossible for those who live from paycheck to paycheck and have little or no safety net of savings to fall back on. If most people quit their jobs tomorrow, they wouldn't have enough money in the bank to pay their bills while they were pursuing even the quickest of the nine options.

There are two typical responses to this dilemma:

• Give up and select option nine—stay where you are.
• Go about the business of starting over while you're still holding down your current job.

The second is so difficult to do that most give up and fall back to staying where they are. The result? What we have now: lots of people who hate their current jobs, would love to start over, but never do it unless forced to by termination.

The worst time in the world to start over is after you've been fired or laid off. That's not because there's a stigma attached to you—so many people are getting pink slips these days that no one thinks twice about it anymore. It's because if you wait until you're terminated to start over, you're beginning unprepared. You'll have no financial cushion other than maybe a severance payment. That traditional two weeks' pay for every year you've worked for a company may have been enough to carry you over to a new job 20 years ago, but it's far from enough today. And it's certainly not enough if you want or need to start over.

Not having a sufficient financial cushion makes starting over much tougher. It decreases the feasibility of every option. It increases the risk of every option. And it turns the time factor into a ticking bomb ready to explode and destroy your life. That's not the best environment for interviewing and networking and thinking. It's clearly not the best environment for sound decision making. The pressure will be on. You're going to choose the most expedient option and take the first job that comes along—just as you did before. And in a few months you'll find yourself right back where you started: hating your job and wanting to start over.

My suggestion is to look at the option or options that appear best after the problem/solution and feasibility/risk/time analyses, see which has the *longest* time factor, and begin setting aside sufficient funds to carry you through that period.

I'm not suggesting you quit your current job as soon as you have sufficient funds. The longer you can stay at your current job while also working at starting over, the better off you'll be: your cushion will be that much more comfortable. And the more comfortable your cushion, the more apt you are to make a sound decision, one you won't end up regretting in six months.

But that doesn't mean you should forgo establishing a sufficient cushion and instead rely on your current stream of income to carry you until you're ready to start over. As soon as you begin the process of starting over you're going to send out signals that something is up. They may be very subtle at first, hardly even noticeable. But as time goes on they'll be more pronounced. At first only your friends at work will notice. Then your peer group will pick up on it. Your immediate superior will soon sense there's something going on. Finally the guy in the corner office will hear about it. Then, when the orders come from the central office to cut staff by 10%, your name will be on top of the list.

It's possible to keep this from happening. But it takes an extraordinary amount of time and effort. In fact, you'd have to follow the exact same path as the guy who has decided to stay put after all. That time and effort is better devoted to starting over. It's better to spend your energy on building bridges to your future than to your past.

My advice is to do the minimum maintenance on your current job necessary to keep you from getting in hot water and, simultaneously, begin building a financial cushion and work on starting over. The idea is to prepare as if you're going to quit your job and then start over, but actually hold on to your job as long as possible. If you do lose your current job before you're ready to start over, at least you'll have gotten a head start and be more financially secure. If you're ready to start over and haven't had to rely on your financial reserve, you'll be able to carry forward that financial cushion and use it to make the rest of your life more secure.

That leaves us with the task of figuring out how much you'll need and getting the money together.

Using your check stubs, tax returns, credit card statements, bank statements, and any other financial records you've kept, determine exactly how much you spend every month. Some expenses will be easy to determine because they're the same amount every month, like your mortgage payment or rent or any regular loan payments or bills. Others vary from month to month, like home repairs, the clothing bill, and auto repairs. Don't forget to include a budget line called "cash" and record there all your withdrawals from the bank and all the money from your paychecks that you don't deposit. For the moment, include monthly amounts for retirement plan deposits and other regular saving plans.

My suggestion is to try to put together a year's worth of records, come up with annual totals for your expenses, and divide those by 12 to come up with your monthly totals. That's the way to come up with the most valid numbers, as well as to make sure you don't forget annual or semiannual expenses, such as insurance premiums and tax bills.

I know it's a lot of work, especially if you're not one for keeping good records. But look at it this way: You're starting over in your career, so you might as well start over in your bookkeeping at the same time. Your tax preparer will thank you for it.

Once you've come up with a monthly expense figure, simply multiply it by the time factor for the option you're leaning toward to come up with how much of a cushion you need.

Step 5: If You Don't Have Sufficient Funds, Get Them.

If you're anything like most of my clients, you'll now find yourself confronting two seemingly impossible tasks. Not only are you thinking of starting over, but now you know that in order to do so you're going to have to set aside more money than you've had in one place since you bought your home. Here's another point in the process where people give up and suddenly think their current job isn't so bad after all.

But there's no need to be so pessimistic. Generating a financial cushion isn't impossible. It just requires some thought and sacrifice.

Basically what you're trying to do is generate a financial surplus. There are three ways of doing this:

• You can increase your income while maintaining your level of expenses.
• You can increase your income and decrease your level of expenses.

• You can maintain your income while decreasing your level of expenses.

The first technique is the most comfortable to do. Rather than requiring sacrifices, it means getting a raise and funneling the amount of that raise into your cushion. However, there's a fundamental problem with this approach, at least for someone who wants to start over. Raises aren't easy to come by these days. To get one you'll have to launch a prolonged aggressive campaign. Once again, this approach is the same as if you had decided to stay where you are. The time and effort involved will keep you from looking to the future.

The second technique has the potential to generate the most money. But once again, it requires tremendous effort that could better be devoted to starting over. And it involves sacrifice as well.

The third technique is one that I think is best for you. Sure, it requires sacrifice, but it won't detract from your efforts to start over, and that's your goal, isn't it? If you don't feel strongly enough about starting over to sacrifice a bit in the present for a better future, then you're not really ready to start over.

CUTTING YOUR EXPENSES TO GENERATE A SURPLUS

I know what you're thinking. For years people have been telling you to take a little bit from each paycheck and put it away for a rainy day. You've meant to do just that . . . but something always came up. Now I come along and tell you that in order to start over you need to start setting aside enough money to carry you through the transition. Since you probably haven't even saved two weeks' salary in the past two years, you're ready to throw this book and your dreams of starting over out the window.

But what's different now is you're doing this for a concrete goal—starting over—not for some abstract goal—being frugal. It's as if you were saving to raise the down payment to buy a home. It's also good practice, because if you're thinking of one of those options that involve a potential decrease in your income, you're going to have to get used to trimming your expenses. Finally, what's also different is I've a slightly unconventional approach to saving money.

FOCUS FIRST ON YOUR FIXED EXPENSES

If you look back at the list of monthly expenses you came up with earlier in this chapter, one thing you'll notice is that you have two types of expenses: those that are the same each month and those that depend on your actions or circumstances. Businesses call these categories fixed and variable expenses.

Your fixed expenses include your rent or mortgage payment, income and property taxes, insurance premiums, and debt service.

Your variable expenses include what you spend on food, clothing, utilities, telephone, entertainment, and travel.

Most people look on those fixed expenses as being etched in stone. They also see that those variable expenses are products of their behavior. So when it comes time to trim their expenses they focus on variable expenses or discretionary spending.

From a long-term perspective this makes sense. By just slightly altering your lifestyle, you'll start saving money. But behavioral changes, no matter how dramatic, aren't going to help you come up with the kind of financial cushion you probably need to start over.

Your attitude toward money and spending is more deeply ingrained and habitual than almost any of your other beliefs. It's formed in infancy and is as hard to kick as heroin. You can do it—but it's tough and won't yield the kinds of immediate results you're looking for. By the time you're close to raising enough this way, you'll probably be either terminated or forced into retirement. In order to generate a financial cushion quickly enough for you to start over in the foreseeable future, you'll need to focus on your fixed expenses.

LOOK AT YOUR DEBTS

If you're like most of my clients, the majority of your fixed expenses are debt related—mortgage payments, car loan payments, credit card balances, and so on.

Start by giving up on further debt. Remove the credit cards from your wallet and start paying cash or writing a check for all purchases. That will bring the result of the transaction—the deduction in your bank balance—into sharp focus and give you a moment to think about it. (According to one recent study, the use of credit cards increases consumer spending by 23%.) Keep a charge card in your wallet for emergencies or for times when you don't want to carry a lot of cash or when a merchant won't accept a personal check.

Turn to the worksheet on page 51 and figure out exactly how much you owe. In the first column write down the name and type of the loan. In the second column write down the total balance of the loan. In the third column write down the interest rate. In the fourth column write down the amount of your monthly payment. (For credit cards with large balances, write down the minimum payment required on your last bill.)

Total the numbers in the second column and you'll see exactly how much you owe. Total the numbers in the fourth column to see how much of your monthly fixed expenses are debt related. To help establish a financial cushion to start over you've got to trim one or both of those numbers.

Consider a home-equity loan. Up to $100,000 of home-equity debt is deductible. By using this money to pay off other, nondeductible loans, you can save a considerable amount of cash each month. Let's say you owe $15,000 on a 14% car loan and another $5,000 on a credit card that charges 19%. Take out a home-equity loan and pay off the car loan and credit cards. You'll still owe $20,000, but you'll be paying only, let's say, 9% interest. And that 9% may actually have the impact of only 6% since it's tax-deductible. Low-interest loans, such as government-sponsored education loans, should be left alone.

Consider refinancing your existing mortgage: it could result in lower monthly payments. How much you'll save depends on the specifics of your situation. But just for an example, if you've a $100,000 mortgage and you're currently paying about 9% interest, your monthly payment is probably about $800. Refinance and get a 7% mortgage and your monthly payment will drop to around $660. That's $140 a month you can save for a total of $1,680 a year. While the standard rule of thumb was to refinance if you could save two or more points of interest, today it makes sense to do the calculations yourself. (You can use the worksheet on page 52.) That's because in slow housing markets lenders sometimes waive their fees and charges and will absorb closing costs. In that case, even a small drop in interest could result in savings. The key question to ask yourself is how long you intend to stay in the house. If you'll be living there long enough for the monthly savings to be greater than the closing costs, it makes sense to refinance. One last thought on mortgage refinancing: While it makes sense to shop around, consider coming back to the holder of your current mortgage with the terms of the best deal you've uncovered. The bank may be willing to match the deal in order to keep your business.

In my experience, by minimizing the amount of money spent each month on debt service, and by turning as much of it as possible into a tax-deductible expense, you'll be able to save between two and three months' worth of expenses over the course of a year.

TRIM YOUR INSURANCE EXPENSES

The next place to look to minimize your fixed expenses are insurance premiums. Most of my clients are very lazy insurance consumers. I think that's because it's a depressing and annoying purchase. Few of them actually shop around for the best coverage. Instead they rely on an agent who was referred by a friend or relative. And almost none of my clients change insurers once they've been signed up. If you want to start over soon, you'd better take a more aggressive approach to your insurance bill.

Begin with health insurance. Calculate how large a deductible you can afford. If you and your spouse can afford to absorb $1,000 in medical bills each, increase your deductible to that level. The higher the deductible you take, the lower your monthly premium will be. For example, increasing your deductible from $100 to $1,000 can cut your premium by 25%.

Think about alternative types of coverage. Most of my clients are reflexively attached to major medical coverage. Health maintenance organizations and health insurance plans, while limiting your options somewhat, can reduce your costs dramatically. While your monthly premiums may actually go up anywhere from $6 to $20 by joining an HMO, the cost of your health care will plummet. Rather than having to make a co-payment of perhaps 20%, you'll pay a flat fee of perhaps $5 for each doctor visit, prescription, or lab test.

Most of my clients have far more life insurance coverage than they need. If you don't have dependents, you don't need life insurance. If you've dependents, you need only enough life insurance to

- pay off your debts;
- cover your funeral expenses;
- take care of outstanding obligations;
- provide your spouse with enough money to replace your income for two to three years (at that point she'll either have increased her own income or changed her lifestyle).

Forget about whole, variable, and universal life—you're buying insurance, not making an investment. Stick with term life insurance. It's cheapest and offers the best coverage.

Examine your disability insurance coverage. Lots of my clients have made the mistake of taking out policies that pay benefits equal to their gross incomes. But benefits on disability policies for which you pay the premium are tax-free. That means you need to receive only your take-home pay. In addition, you can assume you'll be changing your lifestyle and spending less if you're disabled, lowering the necessary benefit even further.

Homeowner's insurance can also be trimmed. Its purpose should be to rebuild your home in case of disaster, not to replace a broken window. Take as high a deductible as you can afford. Increasing it from $250 to $1,000 could cut your annual premium by 20%. Change your policy to cover only the structure, not the surrounding property. Go over your personal property coverage. Insure only the things you can or would replace if lost or damaged. There's no way you could ever replace your great-grandfather's pocket watch, so why insure it?

Finally, take a close look at your auto coverage. Most of my clients have policies for much more than the minimum coverage required by state law. Consider paring back coverage as close to the state requirements as is possible and prudent. If your car is more than three years old, consider dropping your collision and comprehensive coverage. That could cut your premium by 30% to 40%. If you don't want to go that far, up your deductible from $100 to $1,000. That will cut that portion of your premium in half. Scratch some names (particularly that of your teenage son who's away at college) off the list of regular drivers. Make sure you aren't paying both for towing coverage and membership in an auto club. See if your homeowner's policy covers items stolen from your vehicle, eliminating the need for your auto policy to do the same.

I've found that trimming insurance coverage in this manner can result in an annual savings of one to two months' worth of expenses for most of my clients. Added to your debt reduction efforts, this brings your cushion up to between three and five months' worth of money.

NOW FOCUS ON YOUR VARIABLE EXPENSES

Take out that list of monthly expenses you drew up earlier. This time try to figure out where all the cash withdrawals are going. Once you've got a handle on most of those expenditures (almost no one can figure out where every penny goes), start looking to streamline and simplify your lifestyle. Can you save enough money to start over? In answer to that question, let me ask you a series of other questions:

• Can you take the bus or train to work rather than drive?
• Can you launder and iron your own shirts rather than go to the cleaner or laundry?
• Can you start buying clothes as you need them (and I do mean need) rather than as you want them?
• Can you cut down the number of times you dine out each month? And while we're on the subject of eating out, can you trim your tipping and have coffee and dessert at home?
• Can you take books out of the library rather than buy them?
• Can you rent videos rather than go to the movies?
• Can you bring your lunch rather than go out to lunch every day?
• Can you buy magazines at the newsstand, as you finish them, rather than subscribing and letting them pile up unread?
• Can you give baked goods or handmade items as gifts?
• Can you clip coupons and prepare a list before you go food shopping?
• Can you buy generic, store, or regional brands rather than heavily advertised national products?
• Can you compare unit prices?

- Can you buy staples in bulk?
- Can you turn shopping back into a chore rather than a hobby?
- Can you place egg timers by the telephone to remind you to keep calls short?
- Can you turn your thermostat down to 50° when you leave the house in the morning and down to 60° when you go to bed at night?
- Can you turn lights out when you leave the room?
- Can you fill the dishwasher completely before running it, and use energy-saving settings?
- Can you wash clothes in cold rather than warm or hot water and line dry them?
- Can you take showers instead of baths?

I'm not saying you have to do everything I've suggested. However, I have to point out that the more you trim your discretionary spending, the more feasible, less risky, and quicker it will be for you to start over. To put it another way, the more of a financial cushion you're able to build up, the more likely you are to be able to select a riskier, less feasible, but potentially more satisfying option. The power to change your life in the way you want is in your hands.

TOTAL INDEBTEDNESS WORKSHEET

Column #1	Column #2	Column #3	Column #4
Name and Type of Loan	Balance Due	Interest Rate	Monthly Payment

Total of column #2 equals total indebtedness _____

Total of column #4 equals monthly debt service _____

MORTGAGE REFINANCING WORKSHEET

Section A: Potential Savings

1. Current monthly payment _____

2. New monthly payment _____

3. Line 2 subtracted from line 1 equals
potential monthly savings _____

4. Line 3 multiplied by 12 equals
potential yearly savings _____

5. Line 4 multiplied by term of loan
equals total potential savings _____

Section B: Cost of Refinancing

6. Cost of up-front points _____

7. Bank's attorney's fees _____

8. Your attorney's fees _____

9. Bank's application and appraisal fees _____

10. Total of lines 6, 7, 8, and 9 equals
total cost of refinancing _____

Section C: Break Even

11. Line 10 divided by line 3 equals
number of months it takes to break
even _____

Step 6: Pain Versus Gain—the Final Analysis

Whether or not you start over depends on you. All I can do is offer some guidance and advice. I've tried to make this as systematic a process as I could, but from this point on it's an inside job.

Let's look at the most rational and pragmatic way to decide which of the nine options is right for you.

Begin by weeding out those options that won't definitely solve your primary problem. Of the remaining options, choose the one that's the most feasible and the least risky. Finally, build up a financial cushion equal to the length of time it takes to put that option into practice, while keeping your job, and don't do anything until you've got sufficient money in the bank. Such an approach maximizes your chances for ridding yourself of the pain you're experiencing. However, it doesn't maximize your chances of joy.

To do that, you'll have to be a lot more daring and more instinctual. You may have to choose an option that could solve your problem but also might not. You may have to make the leap before you've built up sufficient finances to insure your security. You may have to pursue a less feasible, riskier path. As with many other choices facing you in life, it's a question of pain versus gain.

I need to add one further element into your decision making. Don't feel or act as if you're choosing a course for the rest of your life; you're probably not. With the way our economy is changing it's likely a middle-aged baby boomer who starts over will want to, or have to, start over at least once more in his life. The days of having one career are gone. And the days of having two careers are rapidly coming to an end. By the end of the century it's probable that Americans will have three or more careers during their working lives.

Is the decision you're making important? Certainly.

Is it irreversible? Perhaps, depending on which option you choose.

Is it final? I don't think so. In another five years you're probably going to be picking up this book again, or some other like it, and going through the same process. One cliché that's definitely true is that the only constant in the workplace of the future will be change.

CHAPTER 5

Get Another Job in the Same Career and in the Same Industry

THE FACTS AT A GLANCE

- Feasibility: 2 if you're in a growing industry, 4 if you're in a shrinking industry
- Risk: 2
- Problems it **will** solve: not financially rewarding, maxed out in company, unhealthy environment
- Time: 1 month for each $10,000 you're currently earning

I know. You picked up this book thinking you'd be making some revolutionary change in your life. Now you've ended up with the option that's the most traditional response to job unhappiness and you're feeling as though you've wasted your time. Far from it.

Nearly 25% of my clients end up choosing this option. (Another 50% choose an even less revolutionary step: they stay in the same job.) Reading the first four chapters of this book and going through the exercises I recommended wasn't a waste of time. It opened your eyes to what your actual problems are and what the most rational response should be to those problems.

Most people think it will take some radical change to feel better about their jobs and careers. They see their unhappiness as so dramatic and all-encompassing that only a dramatic act or gesture could possibly turn their feelings around. Actually it's often the simplest thing about a job that's the most troubling. But because most of us look to our jobs as the source of and solution to so many of our problems, personal as well as professional, imagined as well as real, we think radical change is required.

Ending up with this option demonstrates you're not only pragmatic, but you've a keen sense of self. You've been able to admit that what's really bothering you is you're not taking home enough money, you've no place to go in this company, or your current environment is driving you to despair. Getting another job in the same industry and career will not only solve all three of these problems, it will do so in the least risky manner. And if you're in an industry that's growing rather than shrinking, it's highly feasible, too.

There are lots of excellent books on this subject, and I'll suggest some at the end of this book. Since I can't come close to doing justice to such a big subject in one chapter, I'll take a different approach. I'm going to offer my own advice on what I think are the most important elements of finding another job.

First, don't despair. Finding a new job with better compensation isn't impossible. Even though most large companies are continuing to lay off workers, new businesses are starting up and other existing businesses are expanding. In fact, odds are more jobs will be created than lost in the next year. Sure, many of these new jobs will be lower paying and offer fewer benefits than the jobs that are vanishing, but that's not true of all the new jobs.

Lots of good positions in good companies are available for the right candidates. However, they will be in new places, require different work situations, offer different kinds of benefits, and involve acceptance of a new kind of contract between employers and employees.

Make Sure You Look in the Right Places

Large companies are no longer the place to look for new jobs. And since not even they can offer job security or good benefits anymore, there's no reason to even consider them. Open your mind up to new possibilities:

• Look to small- and medium-size companies.
• Look to foreign companies.
• Look to new companies.

Be Open to New Working Situations

At the same time as you're looking in these new places, be prepared to accept a different kind of working situation than you may have been used to at a large company.

• Be prepared to work in teams rather than departments. Companies are much more flexible in structure than in the past, and you've got to be just as flexible.
• Be prepared to work for a woman or minority member. Women are starting business at 1.5 times the rate of men.
• Be prepared to do your own support work. Your staff is your personal computer, the software loaded in it, and the laser printer and modem hooked up to it.

• Be prepared to do without a private office or maybe even any office. You could be a telecommuter whose office is at home. Or you could be an entirely mobile worker whose office is the contents of his briefcase—a laptop computer with built-in fax/modem and a cellular telephone.

Be Open to New Kinds of Benefits and Compensation

Don't expect to find a job with the traditional big company benefit package anymore. Pay will no longer be based on seniority or experience. The days of company cars and fully funded pension plans are over. But new benefits are taking their place. From now on, look for

• pay based on your knowledge, skill, flexibility, adaptability, and, most important of all, performance;
• training and education that adds to your skills;
• opportunities to broaden your experiences and to achieve success in different areas.

Understand There's a New Employer/Employee Contract

Finally, since it's clear to anyone who hasn't had his head in the sand for the past 10 years that the old social contract between employers and employees is dead, you're going to have to accept a new one if you're to find another job. There's a rush on to define this new contract for the twenty-first century. Lots of attempts have been made, but in my opinion the best one so far has come from a study by Kenneth Chilton and Murray Weidenbaum called "A New Social Contract for the American Workplace: From Paternalism to Partnering." Here are the terms they suggest.

Employers agree

- to offer fair pay and benefits linked to employees' contributions to the success of the company.
- that employees' security is tied to the company's fortunes.
- to respect employees, recognize their contribution, and seek their participation.
- to offer opportunities for employees to grow.
- to provide free and open access to information.
- to provide a safe and healthy workplace.

Employees agree

- to perform to the best of their abilities.
- to be committed to the company's goals.
- to participate in the company by offering suggestions.
- to be willing to undergo training to improve their productivity.
- to behave ethically and honestly.

Both employers and employees accept that

- partnering has replaced paternalism as the model for their relationship.
- employees are resources, not costs to be cut.
- their joint focus has to be satisfying customer needs and desires.

Do Not Quit Your Job until You've Lined up Another

This normally would go without saying, but since this is a book for people who are very unhappy with their jobs, I thought I'd say it anyway.

People who are employed are more attractive to potential employers in the same industry than those who are unemployed. Hiring you is a double win for your new employer: not only does he get your services, but he deprives a direct competitor of your services as well.

Perhaps more important, if you're still employed, you'll be more apt to take your time looking for the right job than jumping at the first thing that comes along. The inability to wait for the right opportunity is probably one of the reasons you're in a job you're not happy with right now. Why make the same mistake again?

Keep Your Search a Secret

Obviously the people you contact and meet with will know you're looking for another job. But for your own sake, limit the number of people who know you're testing the waters. As soon as your current employer learns you're looking around, you'll be moved to the top of the list of potential layoffs, you'll be left out of important meetings, and you'll be forever branded as disloyal.

Try to act and look the same as you always do at work. Showing up in a suit when you normally wear jeans and sneakers is a tip-off you're going on an interview at lunch. So too is taking lots of individual sick days or consistently coming in late or leaving early. The secret is to do your interviewing during lunch hours if possible. If not, do it prior to or after normal working hours. If you must take time off work, take entire days and try to schedule more than one interview on that day. Try to have all your job-hunting correspondence sent to your home. Limit calls to your office if possible. You want the fact that you've landed a new job to come as a complete shock to your current employer.

Think of Yourself As a Commodity

The secret of speeding up your job search is to sell yourself like a commodity. If your assignment was to sell a particular car, you'd take a look at it, figure out what makes it good and what are its benefits and features. Then you'd decide how best to tell car buyers about those benefits and features. That's the same process for developing a job campaign . . . except you are the car.

Develop an Achievement-Oriented Résumé

The biggest mistake job hunters make is they don't realize résumés are designed to help the employer, not the employee. They are a negative screening device. Potential employers scan through résumés quickly, looking for something to disqualify the candidate.

They begin by looking for lack of experience and expertise to weed out those who are clearly unqualified. But there are also some subjective analyses. Some executives eliminate candidates from schools or companies they don't like. Others discard résumés of candidates who have worked for one company for too long a period of time or who have jumped from one company to another too often. The goal is to trim the number of potential candidates to a size that's easy to handle.

Therefore the goal of your résumé should be to minimize potential negatives, maximize positive achievements, and, as a result, boost your chances of getting through the screening and being invited for an interview. That's the only purpose of a résumé: to get you an interview. It's how you perform at the interview, not your résumé, that actually gets you the job.

Since most potentially negative factors come from your career chronology, it's better to stress personal attributes and achievements than individual jobs. And your achievements should all focus on the one thing that counts: making the company more money, either by cutting costs or boosting revenues.

Detail your achievements and translate them into dollars and cents. Retrace your career, looking for instances when your efforts and leadership resulted in cost savings or revenue increases. Include specific data, such as percentages, dollar amounts, or lengths of time. If you don't have exact numbers, come up with your own estimates—as long as they don't look impossible, they'll be accepted as true.

Minimize Problems in Your Career Chronology

Even though you're putting together an achievement-oriented résumé you'll still have to include a career chronology. Employers want to know where you've worked and for how long. But place your chronology after your list of achievements, forcing employers to focus on positives rather than potential negatives. You can also minimize potential stumbling blocks by correctly formatting your career chronology.

- Include salary figures and/or job descriptions to show each move in an unusually long series has been made for good reasons.
- If you've been with one company for a long time, demonstrate progression within the company by treating each promotion, change in responsibilities, and salary increase as a separate entry.
- Gaps can be eliminated by explaining how the time was used—to write a book or go back to school, for instance.

Use Your Interests to Your Advantage

Most people view a listing of interests as a throwaway, something to fill up the last bit of white space on a page. That need not be the case. By saying that some form of challenging aerobic exercise is one of your interests, you imply you're a nonsmoker who's in good health—two things an interviewer wants to know but can't ask. By noting you're interested in an analytical game, like chess, bridge, or go, you imply you're a thoughtful problem solver. And by being very specific about other interests, you paint yourself as a more interesting person. For instance, rather than saying you're interested in art, say you're interested in seventeenth-century German portraiture. Who knows, you could come across another enthusiast and get the job right away.

Traditional Appearances Are Best . . . Even for Nontraditional Résumés

Unusual typefaces, colored paper, photographs, videotapes, and other gimmicks are taken as signs of a lack of respect for business norms, not as creativity. Stick to 10- or 12-point serif typefaces printed in black ink on white paper. And try to keep your résumé to two pages or less.

Here's a sample résumé incorporating many of the points I just went over:

Michael Johnson
27 Alameda Drive
Tuscarora, NY 14762
Home: 617/555-7564
Work: 617/555-8765
E-mail: michaelj@aol.com

Career Achievements

- Maintained turnaround time and quality of editorial package at consumer electronics magazine while trimming staff by 25 percent.
- Doubled readership and ad pages through total redesign of consumer photographic magazine while keeping production costs stable.
- Cut production time of professional photographic magazine in half through creation of new format and editorial package.
- Increased productivity of weekly newspaper editorial staff by 60 percent by instituting flexible scheduling.

Career Chronology

- Editor, *Electronic Wonders,* a monthly consumer electronics magazine published by Microchip Media Inc., January 1990 to the present; responsible for supervision and direction of editorial, art, and production staffs.
- Editor, *Photographic Phenoms,* a monthly consumer photographic magazine published by Flashbulb Publications, July 1988 to December 1990; responsible for supervision and direction of editorial and art staffs.

- Completed course work for MBA degree, September 1987 to June 1988.
- Managing Editor, *Photo Retailing,* a biweekly photographic trade magazine published by Photo Retailing Publishing Corp., January 1987 to August 1987; responsible for design and supervision of copy flow and page production systems.
- News Editor, *Seneca Eagle,* a weekly newspaper published by Seneca Eagle Press, August 1983 to December 1986; responsible for management and supervision of full- and part-time reporting staff of 15.

Education

- Bachelor of Arts in American Literature from the State University of New York College at Seneca
- Masters of Business Administration from the State University of New York College at Unadilla

Interests

- Backpacking
- Chess
- Nineteenth-century Russian poetry

Don't Rely on Answering Ads, Bulk Mailings, Employment Agencies, or Headhunters

Relying on Help Wanted ads and bulk mailings to find a job is like depending on lottery winnings to finance your retirement. It could work, but the odds are long. Thousands of other people are looking for jobs in your industry, all answering the same ads and soliciting the same companies. Feel free to answer ads that seem perfect for you. But stretching your definition of perfection will increase the number of rejections you'll receive, not your changes of getting a new job.

Employment agencies and headhunters won't help much, either. Most of them are paid by companies looking to fill positions. They'll probably be in touch with you only when they've got a position you're overqualified for, that pays half what you're making now.

Rely on Networking

About 70% of all job openings are filled through personal contacts. So rather than sending out résumés in response to ads or in bulk mailings, solicit advice and guidance from everyone you know. Telephone both personal and business contacts and tell them, in confidence, you're looking for a new job. Stress you're looking for guidance and advice, and say you're willing to meet with anyone to discuss opportunities.

By opening yourself up to exploratory meetings in this way, you're expanding your network dramatically. I may not know anyone who has any openings, but I could send you to talk to my friend Jim. He may not have or know of any openings, either, but Jim could send you to speak to his friend Frank, who may have, or know of, an opening. You've expanded your network three times just by being willing to chat.

You're not inconveniencing people by asking for these meetings. Business is built on contacts and favors. If I can help you, somewhere down the road maybe you'll help me. And if a friend of mine helps you, he knows I'll help his friend.

Consider Using the Internet

Even though you've chosen a traditional option—looking for another job in the same career or industry—that doesn't mean you shouldn't consider pursuing nontraditional means of finding that job. One of the most sensible uses for the Internet that I've so far discovered is as a worldwide Help Wanted bulletin board. While the Net has been all the rage in the media, it still isn't so heavily traveled as to make a job search on it like looking for a needle in a haystack. However, in my opinion, in a few years it might be no more fruitful than Help Wanted ads. But until then consider browsing the following sites on the World Wide Web (additional sites are listed in the appendices at the back of the book):

- Career Mosaic (http://www.careermosaic.com): will let you search the tens of thousands of postings on the JOBS database and the Usenet newsgroups by keyword or topic.
- E-span (http://www.espan.com): consists of about 10,000 paid Help Wanted ads that can be scanned for free by job hunters. You can key in your own résumé summary and keywords to help uncover possible matches. In addition, you can sign up to have potential leads sent to you via E-mail.
- Job Search and Employment Opportunities: Best Bets from the Net (http://asa.ugl.lib.umich.edu/chdocs/employment/job-guide.toc.html): a compex URL (uniform resource locator—see page 141) for a good site, managed by the University of Michigan's library, that lists nationwide job openings by occupation and category.
- JobWeb (http://www.jobweb.org): job listings are indexed by region and profession, and links are provided to resources such as professional associations and headhunters.
- Monster Board (http://www.monster.com): said to be the biggest job database on the Net with approximately 50,000 listings that can be searched by industry, title, and region. There

are also opportunities to submit your own résumé to a database that can be searched by employers, and to scan a calendar of nationwide job fairs.

- Online Career Center (http://www.occ.com/occ): provides a database of jobs that's searchable by city, state, and industry.
- Career Links (http://www.careertalk.com/career—links. html): offers links to most of the other career- and job-related sites on the Web.

Prepare for Each and Every Interview

Regardless of who recommends you, what Web pages you've browsed, or how great your résumé reads, it's how you come across in the interview that gets you the job. And to come across well you have to be prepared. I don't mean wearing a clean shirt and popping a breath mint. I mean learning everything you can about the company and the interviewer.

If the interview comes as a result of networking, ask the intermediary about the person you'll be meeting. However the interview came about, go to the library and research the company and its place within its industry. Consult newspapers, magazines, and trade journals. Scan the Net for information. If it's a public company, get its three most recent annual reports and read the letters from the chairman and president. Even if you never actually get a chance to use all your information, it will make you more comfortable and that will help you come across better.

During your preparations think about how you'll answer specific questions. These are the 10 questions most often asked by interviewers:

- Why do you want to work here?
- What makes you think you're qualified for this job?
- Why did you leave your last job?

- What are your strengths and weaknesses?
- What are your career and personal goals?
- Where do you see yourself in five years?
- What did you like and dislike about previous jobs?
- How would you characterize your work and management styles?
- Have you ever had to deal with a difficult boss or subordinate?
- What are your general personal and professional accomplishments?

You don't have to memorize set answers to all these questions. You just need to be comfortable answering them so you come across as polished and professional. In answering any questions, be concise and stress your positive traits, abilities, and experiences. Of course, be prepared to address any shortcomings that may come up.

It's also a good idea to prepare a list of questions of your own. Invariably the interviewer will ask you if you have any questions. If you have none, you'll look uninterested, ill prepared, and passive. Here are some questions that will not only make you look good, but will also elicit some valuable information:

- What are the major responsibilities of this position?
- What would you consider the major challenges facing this position?
- Whom does the person in this position report to?
- How much staff support will be available?
- Has the budget for this department been increasing or decreasing?
- What's the work atmosphere like in this company?
- What happened to the person who previously held the position?
- What would you consider the drawbacks to the position?
- What opportunities for advancement are there in the company?
- Where do you see the company headed in the next five years?

Keep right on doing research until the interview actually takes place. For instance, make sure you read the newspaper that morning, since the interviewer may bring up a story in the news and ask how you think it affects the industry.

Turning Rejections into Resources

Don't view rejections as entirely negative. They offer a chance to get some excellent advice and feedback. Write the interviewer a note asking for his help. Say you're interested in refining your interpersonal skills and would be interested if he thought there were any weaknesses in your presentation. Thank him in advance for a response. This could elicit an excellent, unbiased critique. Who knows, you may even be able to add him to your network.

Don't Forget to Negotiate Salary Offers

Simply by taking the advice I've just outlined and getting another job, you'll solve the problems of being maxed out in a company or being stuck in an unhealthy environment. But to increase your income you'll have to become a savvy negotiator as well.

One of the biggest mistakes I see my job-hunting clients make is failing to realize they're engaging in a two-part negotiation: first that they're the right person for the job, and second that they deserve big bucks. Most people concentrate on the former. If they get the job, they feel they're successful. But that's only half the battle—and not even the most important half for those whose problem is they're not making enough money. In order to be truly successful with this option you need to persuade the interviewer that he wants to hire you, negotiate salary, and *then* accept the job.

Starting salary is the factor that plays the most important role in determining your job income. Raises, especially today, don't result in significant increases in salary since they're usually based on percentages.

Employers have a salary range in mind for an open position. If it's a job just vacated, the employer is probably looking to pay what he was paying the last person who held the job. He'd love to pay less, but he'd probably also be willing to pay more if he thought the new job holder would contribute more. If the position is a new one, a specific figure has probably been budgeted for salary. Once again, he'd love to pay less but will pay more to get more.

If the interviewer brings up salary, he wants you to take the job. But don't get too excited. You'll never be in as strong a negotiating position as you are right now. At this moment you're all potential. You've never made a mistake, had a failure, or suffered a setback. You're the living embodiment of the employer's dreams.

Besides simply realizing that you're in a powerful position, there are three secrets to maximizing your salary: don't be the first to name a figure, realize that things other than money are at issue, and don't accept immediately.

"No, after You. . . ."

If you're the first to name a number, the negotiation will be about decreasing it. If the employer is the first to name a number, the negotiation can be about increasing it. Employers will try to get you to name a figure by asking questions like "How much of a salary are you looking for?" Respond with innocuous answers like "I'm looking for a salary commensurate with my experience and skills." Then ask the interviewer, "What salary are you willing to pay the person who takes this position?"

This little dance can go on and on. It's sort of like the old comedy routine in which two people are overly polite about who will go through a doorway first. One says, "After you." The other replies, "No, after you." The politeness ends up leading to a fight. If your dialogue threatens to get this ridiculous, go ahead and name a figure. Just make sure the number you offer is high enough so you've room to negotiate down and still be happy.

In negotiating salary, assume there's a 20% to 25% flexibility—for example, from a low of $80,000 to a high of $120,000, with a midpoint of $100,000. It's also safe to assume that the employer's first offer is in the low end of that range. So if you're offered $40,000, you can comfortably come back with a counter closer to $50,000.

Include Things Other Than Cash in the Negotiation

Compensation is a mosaic of various elements, including things such as titles, tuition reimbursement, and medical coverage as well as salary. All of these things, and more, can and should become part of your negotiation. That's because it's often easier for an employer to come up with these other benefits than it is to increase the salary figure. Just make sure you're actually receiving something that's of material, not just psychic, benefit. For instance, a corner office is of no real value, while tuition assistance can be quite valuable.

Don't Accept Immediately

When you're tempted to accept an offer, hesitate, look the interviewer in the eye, and ask, "Is that the best you can do?" Don't break eye contact or say anything else until he responds. Regardless of his answer, say, "I'm excited about the position, but I'd like to go home and think about everything we discussed." Then ask, "Would it be okay if I get back to you tomorrow morning?" This gives him another chance to up his offer in exchange for your immediate acceptance.

The Story of Matthew Porter

(In this and subsequent chapters I'll be telling the stories of clients of mine who successfully pursued the option in question. I've changed their names and some of the details of their situations in order to protect their privacy.)

When 42-year-old Matthew Porter came to my office in January 1993, he was a pillar of misery. It wasn't his personal life that was getting him down. He and his 37-year-old wife, Wendy, were obviously very much in love—you just had to see her hold his hand as he spoke to see that. They doted on their children, two-year-old Dylan and four-year-old Nikki. Sure, they wished their three-bedroom split-level in a northern suburb of New York City was bigger and was increasing in value rather than stagnating, but they loved the house, the town, and, most of all, the school system. Following a few minutes of conversation with me, Matthew began opening up about his job and career.

After five years as a senior editor at a well-known men's fashion magazine, he was fed up. Matthew got into magazine publishing right after graduating from an expensive private college in Massachusetts. He had worked his way up the editorial ladder over the course of two decades. For the first five years of his career he had jumped from one small magazine to another—the common technique young editors use to advance. Then he landed a job at a very well known publishing company as managing editor of a computer magazine. That was right about the time the personal computer industry was just taking off. Matthew rode the PC wave along with the magazine for eight years, building up his contacts and his skills.

At a trade show out in Las Vegas, Matthew met a young British editor who had just been given the job of editor in chief of a men's fashion and lifestyle magazine that had grown stale and was threatened with extinction. Matthew was impressed by Nigel's ideas, drive, and high-powered connections, even though he seemed a bit short of nuts-and-bolts skills. Nigel was impressed by Matthew's hands-on skills. After a few beers at a hotel bar Nigel offered Matthew the job as his second in command. Basically Matthew would be the "inside man" while Nigel was out promoting the publication to anyone who would listen. It seemed like a match made in heaven—especially since Nigel offered Matthew a 20% raise over what he was making at the computer magazine. Matthew came home from Las Vegas, talked it over with Wendy, and gave notice to his boss at the computer magazine.

For the first five years of his tenure at the new magazine, Matthew was happy and excited about his career. Together he and Nigel, along with a young woman ad sales exec, turned the staid old publication around. Slowly but surely the magazine became the talk of the industry, eventually becoming the number one men's magazine. While all this was going on Matthew was excited and energized. His salary wasn't growing as fast as he'd hoped, but the sense of camaraderie and mission, followed by the feeling of accomplishment, were heady. But once they'd reached their goal, things changed. In fact, for the past two years Matthew had been miserable.

At first he thought it was magazine publishing itself that was getting him down. He said he had to start from scratch each month and was only as good as his last issue. The pressures and stress were enormous, and the financial rewards—at least his financial rewards—weren't. He was making $65,000. But after he and I worked through the exercises outlined earlier in this book, Matthew realized what his real problems were.

Upon examination, Matthew realized he had two major problems. First, he was angry with Nigel. On their way to the top Nigel never hesitated to credit Matthew with being the glue that held everything together. But success had gone to his head. Matthew felt that he was now considered a second-class citizen. Certainly he didn't fit in with the high-flying crowd of media types Nigel was now hanging out with. Nigel was having less and less to do with the actual operation of the magazine and was spending more time promoting himself than the publication. Once quick to share credit, Nigel now took it all for himself. The same was true of the profits. In the early days Nigel made it a point to tell the staff, including Matthew, that they would all share in the magazine's success. But lately everyone's share but Nigel's had been stagnant. That was the second problem.

Matthew wasn't satisfied with his salary. He felt that after 20 years and some proven successes he should be earning more than $65,000—especially since Nigel was earning over $100,000. While his salary sounded like a lot of money to some people, with his commutation, child care, and household expenses it simply wasn't going very far. He was tired of feeling as if he and Wendy still had to watch every penny. And he saw the costs of sending two children to college looming in the distance, not to mention his own retirement.

After just a couple of conversations it was clear Matthew still loved magazine publishing—he just didn't like his current job. I pointed out that by finding another job in the same industry, he certainly would get out from under Nigel's thumb and he might very well be able to increase his salary. Despite his protestations that there weren't many jobs in magazine publishing right now, he acted on my advice to look in unusual places, be open to different work situations, and be prepared for unconventional compensation packages.

After six months of subtle networking Matthew was introduced to the owner of a small French trade magazine publishing company. The company was looking for an editorial director to supervise and improve the content of the 10 American publications the company had just bought. He and Matthew hit if off right away. While he couldn't offer Matthew any more than the $65,000 he was earning at the fashion magazine, he did suggest a telecommuting and flextime arrangement—a pattern the firm had used successfully with its French executives. In addition, he stressed that as the top American in the firm, Matthew would be the primary representative of the company in the States.

While heading up the editorial side of a trade magazine company wasn't as glamorous as working at a well-known consumer magazine, it did have definite advantages. By not having to commute regularly, and by saving on child care costs, Matthew could make it possible for Wendy to take a part-time teaching job to supplement their income. They figured this arrangement was worth another $10,000 a year to them. That was $10,000 that could be invested for the college educations of their children and his own retirement. In addition, there wouldn't be anyone like Nigel to steal his thunder. Matthew took the job. That was 18 months ago. The last time I spoke with him he told me he hadn't been this happy in years.

For More Information

There are many good books on job hunting, résumés, networking, and interviews. You can find a brief list to get you started on your research in Appendix One on page 199.

CHAPTER 6

Get Another Job in the Same Career but a Different Industry

THE FACTS AT A GLANCE

- Feasibility: 4
- Risk: 2 if you're shifting to a growing industry, 4 if you're shifting to a shrinking industry
- Problems it *will* solve: maxed out in company, maxed out in industry, unhealthy environment
- Time: 6 months plus 1 month for each $10,000 you're currently earning

---

For most people today, shifting industries is a reactive rather than a proactive step. Terminated and unable to find a comparable job in their own industry, they look for another industry— either one that values their experiences and skills or simply one that's growing and therefore hiring.

You, however, are starting over, not rebounding from a termination. While you may hate your current job, you're not staring hunger in the face. You have the luxury of making a proactive rather than a reactive choice. And if you analyze the pros, cons, feasibility, and risks associated with this choice, and look at the problems it definitely will solve, I think you'll agree with me that this option makes sense only if your primary problem is that you're maxed out in your present industry.

If that's the case, I can make some assumptions about you.

- Your field isn't considered that important in your industry, but you're probably at least heading a department since you've run out of rungs to climb.
- You've got lots of management experience as well as a high level of skill in your profession.
- You've looked around your industry and realized there are really no other jobs available for you, or at least none that offer more money or influence or responsibility. Any move you made would be a lateral one, and at this point in your life that's not what you're looking for.
- You've read all the articles and books preaching continuing growth and education.
- You know you've reached the point where you could be replaced by someone younger who'd accept a lot less money. They might not do as good a job as you, but in your industry that wouldn't stand in the way of a bottom-line decision.

That's pretty much the classic scenario for industry shifting I've come across with my clients. My advice for someone in this situation is to do two things: first pick a new industry, and then build bridges to it.

Picking an Industry to Target

You don't need to be Faith Popcorn to know some industries will flourish in the coming years while others will stagnate and die.

What are the factors that influence which industries will boom and which will bust? Well, first you can discount personalities and the genius and foibles of individuals. An individual can make or break a company, but not an industry. Sure, Bill Gates is a business genius. But he's not responsible for the entire computer industry rising or falling. He's responsible only for the fortunes of Microsoft.

Similarly I think you can discount economic trends. While individuals aren't powerful enough to impact industries, macro-economic trends are *too* powerful to have a direct effect. These trends will affect cities, states, nations, and continents, but not particular industries. If, heaven forbid, there's a depression, every industry will suffer. Conversely, if there's an economic boom, every industry will do well. I know, some industries are likely to be more affected by an economic trend than other industries, but there's not enough of a difference for me to suggest you use economic trends as a way to select an industry to enter.

(Besides, you can't get any two economists to agree at any one time as to where the economy will be heading in the next quarter, let alone the next five years. If even the experts can't agree on what the trends are or will be, how can you base a decision on them?)

So what trends do affect the health of industries? What trends are the right size and clear enough to help you choose one industry over another? The answer: Demographic and societal trends.

Look at Demographic and Societal Trends

The American population is entering a period of tremendous demographic change, and in business change always offers opportunity. The growth in certain age groups is going to increase the demand for certain products and services and, conversely, decrease the demand for others.

THE ELDERLY POPULATION IS ABOUT TO EXPLODE

Never in the history of the United States have so many people been over the age of 65. The over 50 population will increase 50% in the next 20 years, from 65 million to 97 million. And the number of those over 85 will also soon reach an all-time high.

In addition, these older Americans are members of the wealthiest generation in our nation's history. They started their working lives during the boom period after World War II, and their real estate soared in value during the boom of the early 1980s. They have huge pensions, both public and private, and have been the beneficiaries of incredible government largesse from the GI Bill to Medicare and Social Security.

All that means there will be a lot of well-heeled older Americans in the coming years. Businesses catering to them will do well. What types of businesses cater to a well-heeled older population? I'm sure you can come up with your own list, but let me start you off with mine.

(By the way, in this and in subsequent lists of targets, I'm concentrating on small business-oriented industries, since all indications are that's where most of the new jobs will be in the coming years.)

- Full-service restaurants
- House cleaning services
- Home maintenance services
- Personal services
- Fitness and exercise products
- Vitamins and nutritional supplements
- Toys and games (most of these well-heeled folks will have grandchildren to spoil)

Of course, as this well-heeled group of elders age they're going to need a lot of health care, despite popping vitamins and exercising. The U.S. Bureau of Labor Statistics estimates at least 5% of the American workforce will be working in the health care industry by the turn of the century. And if government cuts back on its share of the health safety net, turning it over to the private sector, it's possible that as much as 20% of us will be working in health care—related businesses by the early 2000s.

The health care—related industries together generate almost $1 trillion (yes, trillion) a year in sales. Home health care alone is generating $12 billion in annual sales and is increasing at a rate of 15% a year. The average elderly person is spending $500 a year on prescription drugs. It's projected that by the end of the century 15% to 20% of the gross domestic product will be spent on health care. So the following industries should certainly be considered prime targets:

- Pharmacies
- Pharmaceutical companies
- Nursing services
- Home health care services
- Nursing facilities
- Professional placement agencies
- Walk-in medical clinics
- Medical practices

BABY BOOMERS ARE GETTING OLDER

America's largest generation, the 76 million baby boomers, are also turning gray. As always, they will remain a lucrative market for goods and services. Better educated than any previous or subsequent generation, they have worldly tastes. Most have created dual–income families to compensate for the fact that their incomes haven't kept pace with their expenses and desires. They married later than their parents and had their children later. They're looking at a middle age that involves young children and college tuition bills without the kinds of federal loan programs their parents were able to use. Still, they dote on their children and value all sorts of education. They're also health conscious and environmentally aware. What business and industries will do well catering to graying baby boomers?

- Fast–food restaurants
- Recreational and less taxing sport businesses (golf, sailing, and walking, for instance)
- Optical aids (lots of reading glasses are going to be sold in the coming years)
- Personal services
- Home maintenance services
- Home cleaning services
- Educational services for children
- Vitamins and nutritional supplements
- Fitness and exercise

THERE IS A BABY BOOMLET

Since 1985 the number of children born each year has increased by one hundred thousand a year. The birth rate in 1990 was actually higher than in 1950. The U.S. Census Bureau estimates that by 2010 the number of minors in the country will have grown around 10%. That's because the youngest members of the baby boom generation are making babies at a rate that matches or exceeds their parents'. While this baby boomlet will never equal the numbers of the boomers, it will have a powerful impact on American society and business. Obviously industries and businesses that cater to children will do better.

For example, 60% of working women today have children under six. By the year 2000 the percentage is projected to rise to 75% thanks to the baby boomlet. Today more than $13 billion is spent on child care–related services. That's going to soar in the coming years.

- Child care
- Educational services for children
- Recreational activities for children
- Children's clothing
- Toys and games

Examine Societal Trends

Along with these three demographic trends there are three societal trends that I think are worth looking at closely. Each also has the power to dictate which businesses and industries will do well and which won't in the coming years.

THE NUCLEAR FAMILY IS NO LONGER DOMINANT

Whether you sided with Dan Quayle or Murphy Brown, there's no denying the facts. The traditional family structure of a dad who worked outside the home, a mom who stayed home and did housework, and two or three kids and a dog is no longer the rule. Instead there are all sorts of permutations: singles of both sexes living alone, single parents of both sexes, gay and straight working couples without children, dual-income gay and straight couples with children. I could, of course, go on and on.

In the context of this chapter, what's important about this trend is that it will have a negative impact on any businesses or industries that target the now vanishing traditional family. For instance, I don't think a lot of waffle irons will be sold in the coming years. In today's families you'll either grab a frozen waffle and microwave it, or if it's the weekend, you'll all head over to Wally's Waffle Hut.

BUSINESS DOWNSIZING WILL CONTINUE

Businesses will continue to shrink in size, farming out all but their core functions, cutting all but the minimum number of staff people. All this will be in an effort to get as close as possible to what's called "a virtual corporation."

Think of a movie production company. It has a core handful of full-time employees. When it starts making a movie it hires electricians, cameramen, writers, directors, actors, stuntpeople, caterers, and on and on. When production ends it reverts to its core group.

Or look at the Rolling Stones. Every five years or so they go on a worldwide concert tour. It's a huge undertaking involving the assembling, disassembling, and movement of hundreds of

84

people and tons of equipment over and over again, around the world, for about a year. Before the tour begins the corporation consists of the four long-term members of the band. When the tour starts the staff expands to hundreds of employees. When the tour ends it goes back to the four members of the band.

Obviously, very few businesses will be able to get down to the size of these two examples, but that won't stop them from trying. And in that effort there are opportunities, opportunities that will be seized on by certain other businesses and industries.

Any business or industry that provides ancillary services to other businesses or industries will do extremely well in the coming years.

- Secretarial services
- Computer services and consulting
- Employment agencies
- Temporary help agencies
- Accounting and bookkeeping services
- Photocopying and printing services
- Graphic art and photographic services
- Public relations firms
- Advertising agencies
- Mailing and postal services
- Office cleaning and maintenance services
- Freelance professionals
- Business consultants
- Legal counsel and advice
- Outplacement services

THE INFORMATION AGE HAS DAWNED

The Internet—the much talked about electronic superhighway—began as a computer network called ARPANET created by the Defense Department in the 1960s to link all the businesses, institutions, and organizations working with it.

After a while some educational institutions in the network began to use the system to talk to each other about their research. By the 1980s personal computers and electronic workstations were everywhere in the universities, so more and more individuals could use the system.

Those employees of universities and large corporations and federal agencies are still a large part of the system. But they've been joined by private individuals who pay services like CompuServe, Prodigy, and American Online for access to the Internet. Lately more and more commercial businesses are getting onto the Internet, particularly using a section of it called the World Wide Web, which allows them to promote and sell products and services.

Learning to use the Internet takes time, but it's getting easier every day thanks to the efforts of on-line services and software engineers. When a person gains access and begins to feel comfortable, they're usually struck by what's now at their fingertips. They can access the holdings of major libraries. Databases worldwide are available, and information can be obtained on virtually every subject imaginable. And people can communicate with one another. If they have the right equipment, they can even see each other.

At the moment, despite all the hype, the vast majority of individuals on the Internet are upper middle class and highly educated. It's more of an exclusive, very expensive, private toll road than a free, public interstate highway. But it's in the best interests of all the commercial elements involved in the Internet to expand that reach and get as many individuals as possible on board. Soon everyone technologically aware and competent enough to use either call waiting or an answering machine will be on the Internet.

What does this mean for you? To be honest, I don't really know. No one else does, either. But I *do* know it will mean *something*. It's becoming increasingly clear that it's this vast shapeless thing called the Internet, rather than a piece of hardware or software technology, that's going to be at the center of the information age. And every industry will have to use it or deal with it in the future. The success an industry has in this effort will impact its health in the coming years. All I can suggest is that you remain aware of this amorphous force out there and watch for developments.

Look for Commonalities among the Trends

My suggestion is that at this point you begin looking for industries that will be positively impacted *by more than one* of the six trends we've just discussed. Read the list over and over. Look for threads that are running through it. Then look for businesses or industries that are positioned to take advantage of these trends.

Sure, it's possible that an industry or business could boom thanks to just one of these trends. However, that's a bit of a risk. It's a lot safer to bet on an industry or business that will boom because of two, three, or four of these trends.

A few industries clearly are in good shape for the future. Health care–related business, for instance, can take advantage of both the growing elderly population and the aging baby boomers. So can fitness and exercise businesses, personal services, home maintenance services, home cleaning services, and vitamin and nutritional supplement businesses. Any child–related industry appears to be positioned to do well since all three demographic trends point toward its future growth. And of course, any business that services these industries will do well thanks to the trend toward downsizing and outsourcing.

Factor Yourself into the Picture

Just because a business or industry is positioned to succeed doesn't mean it's necessarily right for you. That's why the next step is to factor in your own needs, goals, and experiences.

- Is it an industry you'd enjoy working in?
- Does it fit your lifestyle?
- Does it fit your work style?
- Can you apply any of your previous experience to this industry?

To learn the answers to those questions you're going to have to become a student of the industry. You have to become completely up on what's happening in it, what's affecting it, who the players are, what the problems are, and proposed solutions to those problems.

Find a college nearby that offers an MBA program. If none are convenient, look for a school with a well-respected undergraduate business department. Buy a notebook and head over to the business school library. Seek out the reference librarian. Tell him the industry you're interested in learning about. He can refer you to trade publications that cover that industry in particular as well as indexes of articles on the industry in the general business press. Don't feel as though you need to read every article on this first visit. Just get an idea of what resources are available and get your feet wet. Subsequent visits can be devoted to in-depth study.

Either take copious notes or make lots of photocopies and highlight important points. Make sure to get the names, addresses, and telephone numbers of the editors of the leading trade magazines and those of any general business reporters who cover the industry regularly. They'll be a big help later when it comes to establishing a network.

All this research should provide you with the answer to those four questions about how well you and the industry match up.

But it should also justify your selection of it as a growing business, provide you with an idea of who the major players are, and give you an idea of the major issues facing the industry. Before you go any further take a few minutes to write down some thoughts on these three subjects.

Networking in a Foreign Industry

You're going to get a job in this industry the same way you would in your own industry: by networking. But in this case you're going to have to use the side and back doors.

The side door is through your standing as a professional. As soon as you can, get involved in your professional association. It doesn't matter if you've never showed up for a meeting or spoken with anyone there. Call up the president, introduce yourself, and get active. Volunteer. Speak at meetings. Mingle at cocktail parties. If you're a dedicated schmoozer, you should be able to solidify some contacts after a month. Ask these contacts for the names of any members of the professional association in the industry you want to enter.

As soon as you get a name, call and ask for an informal informational meeting about the industry. Drop the name of the person who recommended them, explain you too are a member of the professional association, and ask for just 15 minutes at a time at their convenience.

At this meeting interview the contact as if you were a reporter, not a job seeker. In fact, don't even mention that you're looking for a position. Just say you're interested in the industry and want to learn more about it. Drawing on the information you gathered at the library, discuss the major problems facing the industry, who the players are, and what the future holds. Ask them about what it's like to practice your shared profession in this industry. Try to get a feel for how your experiences and skills could be relevant. Rather than asking if they know of anyone who's looking for someone like you, simply ask them for the name of someone else to speak with about the industry. When you return home, immediately write out a thank-you note, and as soon as you finish licking the stamp, call the new name and start the process all over again. Keep working this side door networking while you also pursue the back door route.

Back door networking is through the press. Contact the editors and writers whose names you culled from your research at the library. Introduce yourself as a professional who's interested in learning more about the industry. Express your admiration for their writing and reporting, citing one or two specific articles. Ask if you can take them to lunch and speak with them about the industry. Use the same tactics as when you spoke with your professional contacts. Again, finish up by asking for yet another person to speak with.

After each informational interview go back to the paragraphs you wrote about justifying your selection of the industry as a growing business, who the major players are, and what are the major issues facing the industry. Update, edit, and refine your entries as you learn more.

Tailor Your Résumé

After a few rounds of side and back door networking you'll have a very good sense of how you and the industry match up. The next step is to make that linkage clear in a newly drafted résumé.

Don't use your old résumé as anything more than a source for addresses and dates. Start from scratch. Pull out your list of problems facing the industry. Rephrase them in generic terms and see which you've solved in your own industry. Now put them back in the new industry's jargon. Voilà! You've just shown how your skills and experiences are transferable to this new industry. In addition, subtly show that you're not only a problem solver, but also a team player. (For more information on résumés see Chapter 5.)

Start bringing your new résumé with you on informational interviews. Make calls to your prior contacts and ask them if they'd take a look at your résumé, just for advice and suggestions, of course. Take whatever advice is offered seriously and show how you've incorporated it by presenting a new draft.

Eventually such dedicated networking should lead to some meetings that involve potential job opportunities. If after two months you haven't yielded any such quasi job interviews, start your networking cycle over. But this time say directly that based on all the wonderful things you'd heard about the industry, you've decided to try to come on board. Ask for help and suggestions.

Interviewing for a Career Shift Job

Once you've shifted from informational interviews to job-related interviews, a subtle shift may also take place in the way the meetings are conducted. Rather than being relaxed, friendly gatherings, they could become a bit more tense and confrontational. That's because as soon as someone has the potential of being an employee it's psychologically important for the other person, in this case the interviewer, to assert his dominance.

You can survive even the most annoying interview if you keep three things in mind:

• Your résumé has already convinced someone that your skills and experiences are indeed transferable. Otherwise you wouldn't have gotten the interview. This meeting is just a way to confirm what they saw in your résumé.
• You must have a rationale for shifting industries. It's not

enough to be coming from an industry in decline and going to an industry on the rise. You need to demonstrate your excitement for this new business. That should be no problem since you've already prepared a written description of why you're attracted to this business.

- How are your skills and experiences transferable? I know you've made the case in your résumé. But you're going to have to make the case again and again through a round of interviews just to make sure that everyone gets the point.

Be prepared for a long cycle of research, side and back door networking, informational interviews, and job interviews. This is going to take time. It's an uphill fight that only you can wage. To win you're going to have to become a master salesman. But it can be done.

The Story of Amy Greenberg

Amy Greenberg first came to my office early in 1995. A charming and engaging 38-year-old single woman, she was quick with a joke and a smile for everyone in my office. Amy was a real pro. The art director of a children's book publishing company, she was well-known and respected in the industry she had served for 15 years. Outwardly she was a pillar of confidence and security. She had carved out a life and career for herself as an independent, successful woman. But after an exchange of pleasantries in my office, her tough-as-nails exterior cracked wide open.

Swallowing tears and a few sniffles, she began telling me about her insensitive and brutal boss. After having gone two years without an increase in salary, Amy had approached her CEO about increasing her compensation. In not so many words she was told she wasn't worth any more.

After comforting her, I began taking her through the exercises outlined earlier in this book. We talked about her industry, the pay scales for her field, and the opportunities she had for advancement. It was then that she realized her problem wasn't her brutally frank boss. Sure, he was insensitive and harsh . . . but he was also right. In her industry she had reached the top spot. No other art director in children's book publishing earned more than the $75,000 she did. Her real problem was that she had maxed out in her industry.

Over the course of two months she and I went over the points I've outlined in this chapter. After analyzing target industries—including other branches of book publishing—Amy decided to pursue the computer game industry, whose customers had similar demographics to those she'd targeted at her publishing job. She reconnected with the art directors guild in her city and began networking at its monthly meetings.

Because she'd put out the word, she was introduced to the art director of a computer game company who came to speak at one of the guild's monthly dinners. He met with her for lunch, told her about the business, and took a look at her portfolio. He then put her in touch with others in the business. After about seven "informational" interviews she was put in touch with the vice president of marketing of an up-and-coming company. They hit it off and she was offered a job. She's making a little bit less than what she was earning in book publishing ($70,000), but now she's got lots of opportunities for future growth and movement in an industry that's growing in leaps and bounds.

For More Information

For sources of information on trends in American society, take a look at Appendix One on page 199.

CHAPTER 7

Get Another Job in the Same Industry but a Different Career

THE FACTS AT A GLANCE

- Feasibility: 4 if you're in a staid industry, 3 if you're in a creative industry
- Risk: 3.5
- Problems it **will** solve: not emotionally, psychologically, or spiritually rewarding; maxed out in company, no longer challenging, unhealthy environment
- Time: 12 months plus 1 month for each $10,000 you're currently earning

---

I think it's important I start this chapter by talking about the definition of career. Obviously, as you can see from the numbers above, we're not talking about shifting from being an accountant in the auto industry to being a lawyer in the auto industry. (To change professions in that way you'll have to go back to school—see Chapter 11.) Instead I'm looking at career changes in terms of business disciplines and organizational roles.

Changing Business Disciplines

In terms of business disciplines there are really only three careers: finance, marketing, and management. The kind of move I'm describing in this chapter would be a shift from the accounting department of a software design firm to the sales department of a software design firm or, more generally, a shift from finance to marketing.

It's always easier to shift *from* finance and management *to* marketing than vice versa. That's because it's easy to demonstrate creativity. It's harder to demonstrate financial or managerial competence without a track record.

It's also easier to shift *from* finance *to* management than vice versa. That's because most financial positions require some management skill, while not all management positions require the kind of financial expertise demanded of a specialist.

The career path based on this business discipline model was for a young person to get an education in all three disciplines, but to major in one of them. He would then get an entry-level job in his chosen discipline and move up a hierarchy based on seniority as much as skill. If the discipline he was in was the one most valued by the organization, he might have a chance at the organization's top spot. If not, his ultimate goal would be to become a vice president of his discipline.

All this is what always led me to tell young people interested in business to start in the finance area, since it provided the easiest spot to shift from if they wanted or needed to shift careers. It was also the discipline from which came most of the upper-level executives.

This three-tracked definition of career has been around for as long as people have viewed business as a discipline to be studied. While it's as much an academic as an organizational division, it's an approach that may continue to work in traditional, conservative industries and companies.

However, I think that if you're interested in maintaining a career into the next century, you'd do better looking at career changes and your career path in a different, newer sense.

Organizational Role Changes

In today's corporate world, career has a new definition. The traditional finance/management/marketing view worked well when organizations were huge pyramids with lots of workers and middle managers. Now that organizations are trying to streamline and downsize, a new view is required. This new approach says there are four careers: strategist, resource provider, project manager, and specialist.

- Strategists are those upper-level people who set the long-term directions for a company or organization. They are the handful of CEOs, presidents, and chairpersons who sit atop the new organizational chart.
- Resource providers are the people who find, develop, and/or manage a resource pool, whether it's money, a staff of experts, or a directory of outside freelancers. These are the CFOs, VPs of marketing and engineering, directors of human resources, and art directors. The better they are at recruiting and managing resources, the more they'll be in demand and the more they'll be paid.
- Project managers are the individuals who are given assignments by the strategists. Project managers turn to the resource providers for the tools they need to get the job done, but they

assume responsibility for accomplishing the goals of the organization. The better project managers are at forming and leading successful teams, the more they'll be in demand and the more they'll be paid.

- Specialists are the talented and skilled individuals who actually do the work of the organization. They nominally report to the resource provider but spend most of their time working with project managers on assignments. The more skilled they are in their specialty, the more they'll be in demand and the more they'll be paid.

Rather than being a move from one discipline to another, today's career shift is a change from one role to another. For example, a specialist can become a resource provider, overseeing a staff of his former peers and in the process becoming more of a supervisor and manager than a practitioner. Or a specialist can become a project manager, marshaling the efforts of a group of varied specialists and in the process becoming more of a leader than a practitioner. The most successful project managers may one day become strategists, setting the goals for other project managers.

Choosing a Career Path

Today's career path is really a choice between remaining a specialist or becoming a generalist.

Someone who decides to remain a specialist is banking on his being and remaining among the best at what it is he does. He's relying on his specialty's continued value to businesses. He's committed to improving his skill above all else.

Someone who decides to become a generalist uses his specialty as the foundation for a mosaic of skills. He becomes good enough at what he does to get noticed, learns how a company generates profits, comes up with ideas based on this knowledge, pushes to get assignments, and has the people skills to lead a successful team.

Since income will be based on effectiveness and value to the organization rather than seniority, the choice between being a specialist or a generalist is an inside one, based on self-analysis.

Remaining a specialist and succeeding requires more of a self-reliant entrepreneurial personality. You'll have to like the idea of being a hired gun and relying on your own abilities. You'll be measuring your progress by how much your skill is improving. You'll seek and take new jobs based on whether they offer you the chance to improve your skills.

Becoming a generalist and succeeding requires being more of a people person. You'll have to like the idea of selling your projects to the bosses and managing team members. You'll be measuring your progress by how valuable the projects you're leading are to the company. You'll seek and take new jobs based on whether they offer you the chance to lead more important projects.

If you've read the previous two sections of this chapter and are still set on changing careers but staying inside your industry, I can safely assume you're looking either to shift from one business discipline to another or to shift from being a specialist to a generalist. Rather than conducting a traditional job search (as outlined in Chapter 5), I'd suggest you try to transfer within your company or get a career mentor.

Transfer within Your Company

The people who should have the most respect for your innate skills and abilities are those for whom you're already working. If you're at a company that's large and/or open-minded enough to encourage transfers among disciplines or roles, I'd suggest you try that before looking outside.

Begin by creating a power base in your new discipline or among the project managers. Speak with those already in the career you'd like to enter. Create relationships with them. Pick their brains. Socialize with them. Express your admiration for what they do.

If your company is officially open to transfers, make public your desire to shift careers. Stress that you love the company and feel that you're ready to use more of your skills to help it. Since you're already known to those you'd like to join, you're less apt to be seen as a threat.

If your company isn't open to transfers or isn't large enough to have experience with career shifts, you'll have to be more covert. Look for voids and vacuums in the area you're seeking to enter. Come up with suggestions and ideas, put them in writing, and submit them to whoever has the power to enact them. If one of your ideas is accepted and you're given the ball to run with, you're on your way to shifting careers, even if it's an evolutionary rather than revolutionary change.

But even if your ideas aren't accepted, or they're handed off to someone else, don't despair. Keep developing them and submitting them. Eventually your persistence will generate a conversation about your continuing efforts. At that point make your feelings known. Once again, stress your love of the company and your desire to do more for it. Express your eagerness to expand your skills into this new area, part-time if need be. If you're given the chance, you're on your way to a new career. If you're not, continue offering suggestions but look to the next technique.

Get a Career Mentor

If you can't use your current employer to shift careers, you'll have to use a less direct path to a new career.

Again, start by building a power base in your chosen career, but this time look both inside and outside your company. Try to be subtle, using industry associations and organizations for your networking outside the organization.

Revise your résumé to demonstrate that you already have the skills this new career demands and, in fact, have much the same experience, albeit in different garb. If there's not enough in your résumé for you to draw on to make these arguments, solicit projects inside and outside your job that will give you the background. For instance, your successful efforts at organizing and managing a charitable drive or political campaign show you've got what it takes to be a project manager.

Once you've got something tangible for your résumé, seek out a career mentor. This should be someone, either inside or outside your company, who's already a success in the career you want to enter. Your goal is to have him attest to your ability to do the same thing he does. In effect you're borrowing his track record. Ask him to prepare a letter that simply but eloquently offers his opinion that you've got the experience and skill to be successful in the same career he's in. The more he cites the same arguments offered in your résumé, the better. This letter should be used in closely targeted job hunts, not in industry-wide broadcasts.

Obviously this process has to be somewhat confidential. Select a career mentor based not only on his abilities, but on the quality of your personal relationship. Only a friend or someone who owes you a favor can be counted on to do this and keep quiet about it.

As you can tell from my timing estimate (12 months plus one month for each $10,000 you're currently earning), neither of

101

these techniques will work overnight. Both require serious and constant effort for more than a year. But if this is truly the option that's best for you, that's not too high a price to pay.

The Story of Nicholas Stern

Twenty-eight-year-old Nicholas Stern jokes that he's a third-generation accountant. Both his grandfather and father were CPAs, and it was almost a given that he'd study accounting and finance when he went to college. Upon graduating from a state university and passing the CPA exam, Nicholas passed up a spot in his father's suburban practice and landed a job in the finance department of a new cable television channel. For the first five years of his career there, things went well. But then he began to get bored. That's when he came to see me.

After he spoke for about an hour, it became clear that Nicholas had chosen finance because of his family's history, not his own interest. While he did have a flair for numbers—perhaps it was genetic—he craved more excitement than the number crunching he was doing and wanted a chance to express his creativity. That was why he'd jumped at the chance to work in television rather than settling into the kind of small company/ tax-planning work his father did. But at the same time he was enough of a pragmatist that he didn't want to throw away the investment he'd made in his career or give up his $50,000 salary and corporate benefits, especially not when he and his wife, Linda, were expecting their first child. Working together, Nicholas and I plotted a subtle campaign to get him transferred to the marketing branch of the cable channel.

Nicholas kept up with his number crunching and made sure his current supervisor knew he remained loyal by consciously eschewing credit and passing it along to his boss. In fact, he worked harder at his current job than ever before. But at the same time, before and after regular working hours and on the weekends, Nicholas prepared suggestion memos.

He began stopping by the marketing department's offices, chatting with the staff. He sought out marketing people at the company gatherings and meetings—even at the softball games. He made it clear that he wasn't trying to undercut anyone, just doing his best for the company's success. At first the marketing staff was suspicious, but after a while they accepted his motives. It didn't hurt that Nicholas always asked questions first and listened carefully to their answers. There was always some connection to finances in his memos, but they became more and more marketing oriented. While most of his ideas were turned down, a couple were given high marks and passed on to the marketing VP for further study.

After about a year of this he approached the president of the channel and directly asked for a shift. The president, familiar with Nicholas's work in finance and some of his suggestions, was eager to inject a financial sense into his marketing department. He agreed to the shift.

Only six months after making the shift, Nicholas has become firmly ensconced in his new field. As luck would have it, his channel was bought by a larger media company known for its bottom-line focus. His financially savvy marketing ideas have become a big hit. His joy at being in a more creative part of business has only recently been topped by the birth of his daughter, Danielle.

For More Information

For sources of more information on changing careers, see Appendix One on page 199.

CHAPTER 8

Get Another Job in a Different Career and a Different Industry

---

THE FACTS AT A GLANCE

- Feasibility: 5+
- Risk: 5
- Problems it **will** solve: maxed out in company, maxed out in industry, no longer challenging, unhealthy environment
- Time: 6 months to get an entry-level job, 24 months plus 1 month for each $10,000 you're currently earning to get a job at close to the same salary you're making now

---

I admire your idealism, drive, and determination. But as your long-distance financial adviser I've got to inject some cold hard facts into your dreams. Looking for a *job* in a different career *and* industry is the least feasible, riskiest, and most time-consuming option you have. I hate to throw cold water on your dreams, but the odds are it's going to take you a long time and lots of effort to land a job that requires you to take an incredible reduction in salary.

As your financial adviser I'd strongly encourage you to reconsider the other options. If you're set on making this kind of dramatic change, how about buying a franchise or an existing business in this new field rather than trying to get a job in it? Believe it or not, those approaches, while equally risky and initially more costly, are far more feasible and more likely eventually to pay off financially.

If I haven't been able to dissuade you and you're still determined to pursue this option, I feel duty-bound to offer some suggestions and information.

Training versus Experience

First, determine whether the skill you need to acquire in this new field is obtained through training or developed through experience.

If it's obtained through training, find yourself a training program, take it, and rely on the program to place you in a job. For more information take a look at Chapter 11, which discusses going back to school.

If it's developed through experience, you're going to have to get an entry-level job in the field. That's going to be very difficult. Sure, you've got lots of life experience and maturity going for you. But if I'm looking for a trainee, why would I want someone who's going to bring his or her own prejudices to the position? I want a clean slate, not a blackboard that's filled with years' worth of opinions and beliefs. Besides, training is an investment in the future. When I teach a bunch of trainees the business from the ground up, it's with the hope that some of them will move into other positions in my company. I'm training my company's future. If you're not young anymore, you're not going to be my company's future.

Combating Age Discrimination

Is this age discrimination? Yes. Can you do anything about it? Not much. You're asking someone—in this case a recruiter—to take as big a risk as you're taking. Why would he do that? Sure, you may be able to make a wonderful case for the magical qualities of maturity and experience, and document your flexibility and adaptability. But when push comes to shove that's not going to cut it. Recruiters aren't paid to take chances.

There are only two things that could make him take the chance: he's your brother-in-law, or your father will throw him $100,000 in business if he hires you.

I'm serious. Nepotism and business bribery are the best ways to get an entry-level job when you're well past the typical age and you're way overqualified. I know that's not the answer most people want to hear, but it's the truth.

It's very hard to prove age discrimination, even in wrongful termination suits. It's even harder to prove it in hiring situations. There could be a million other justifiable reasons a recruiter could cite as to why he didn't hire you for the job. They can range from the obvious (lack of experience) to the obscure (your shoes weren't shined). And not even your own dream team of lawyers could prove the real reason was your age.

The Best and Worst Jobs

If you're daydreaming about what industry or career you'd like to enter, I'd strongly suggest you look at *The Jobs Rated Almanac* by Les Krantz (World Almanac, 1992). Krantz rates jobs on six pragmatic criteria: day-to-day working conditions, income, the outlook for continued employment opportunities, physical requirements, security, and stress.

Based on those criteria the 10 worst jobs are dancer, roustabout, taxicab driver, construction worker, fisherman, roofer, auto painter, seaman, lumberjack, and cowboy.

The 10 best jobs, according to Krantz, are computer systems analyst, actuary, software engineer, accountant, mathematician, computer programmer, parole officer, paralegal, medical secretary, and records technician.

It's interesting to note that the worst all involve heavy physical labor, while the best are all information oriented.

The Story of Mickey Pounds

I can't relate the tale of a client of mine who has pursued this option and succeeded, since I urge them all off this path. However, I can tell you about Mickey Pounds, a business associate of mine.

Mickey was a savvy young lawyer. While he knew the law, Mickey's real gift was in getting along with people. He had a great sense of humor and a real way with words. Clients just loved him. He was being groomed to be a "rainmaker" at a Chicago-based law firm I sometimes worked with. That meant he was going to focus on bringing in new business rather than actually "doing" legal work. Such "rainmakers" are always in demand and tend to move up the partnership ladder very quickly. They're also much sought after by other firms. All that spells big bucks and great perks.

Mickey was married to a lovely woman named Naomi. Smart, sophisticated, and driven, Naomi had a top spot at an advertising agency in Chicago. They had a lovely apartment on Lake Shore Drive and led, to all appearances, an exciting urban life.

But just when everything seemed to be coming up roses for the two of them, Mickey began expressing doubts about his chosen profession. They weren't open, but in his few serious moments when he wasn't performing, it was clear he was unhappy. To those who knew him well it seemed as though he were simply going through the motions. For Mickey that was often enough. But after a few lunches and telephone conversations he finally revealed to me that he wanted to leave law and become a stand-up comic.

I knew that Mickey had dabbled in comedy, going to open-mike nights at local comedy clubs, but I had no idea how strongly he felt about it. Ever the pragmatist, I tried to work out some kind of plan for Mickey to achieve the spirit, if not the details, of his goal. Maybe he could go into entertainment law, I suggested, or work as an artist's agent. Perhaps he could open a nightclub. Why not do his comedy part-time while still working as an attorney? But nothing I said could shake Mickey from his dream. Finally, two weeks after his fortieth birthday he announced to his friends, and Naomi, that he was quitting the firm to become a full-time comic.

He and I stayed in touch for a few years after he left the law. His circumstances changed dramatically, as you might imagine. At first Naomi had a hard time understanding Mickey's decision. Then she gamely offered to support him while he pursued his dream. They kept the Lake Shore Drive apartment for a few months but soon realized they couldn't afford it on just Naomi's salary. Their lifestyle changed along with their address. Naomi was working harder than ever, knowing she was now the breadwinner. That meant going into work earlier and staying later. Mickey pounded the pavement and was able to land some gigs, but of course they were all at night. They were seeing less and less of each other. Despite their best efforts and mutual affection, it was clear that they were heading in opposite directions. They separated and divorced shortly thereafter.

Even after their split, Mickey and I stayed in touch. Whenever we spoke he always said he was happy, though I couldn't tell if he was acting or telling the truth. Starting over in a new, totally different field at the age of 40 changed Mickey's entire life. With the decline in the number of comedy clubs, Mickey shifted gears yet again. The last I heard he had moved out west and was trying to get a job as a joke writer for a television personality. I hope he's happy. I know he's "following his bliss," but I still can't help feeling he made a mistake: there had to be some middle ground that, while perhaps not as satisfying emotionally, could have been more practical.

For More Information

I readily admit I'm not the best source for information on finding out what your dream job would be. If that's what you're looking for, take a look at Appendix One on page 199.

CHAPTER 9

Start Your Own Business in the Same Industry

THE FACTS AT A GLANCE

- Feasibility: 1
- Risk: 5
- Problems it **will** solve: not rewarding emotionally, maxed out in company, maxed out in industry, no longer challenging, unhealthy environment
- Time: 9 to 12 months for an original business, 6 to 9 months if you buy a franchise or an existing business

---

Perhaps the best thing to come out of the traumatic changes in the job market is the resurgence in entrepreneurship. More and more Americans are going into business for themselves. Sure, some are turning to entrepreneurship as a last resort—they can't find a job, so they're starting their own company. But I think most of the new entrepreneurs are people like you who see there are opportunities in this new environment; opportunities to better their emotional, psychological, and perhaps even financial lives; opportunities to start over.

If you've turned to this option, I'll bet you're someone who, while successful in your career or industry, is a bit bored by it all. All the positives about your current career are increasingly outweighed by a sense that you're wasting your time and energy and creativity working for someone else.

When you went through the earlier chapters I bet you uncovered that your primary problems are you're no longer feeling challenged and you're not feeling emotionally, psychologically, or spiritually satisfied. You like the work you're doing, you just want to do it your way and to reap the psychic and financial rewards for your efforts.

You're not alone. Entrepreneurship is booming. How big a trend is it?

- According to the Department of Commerce 14.3 million business tax returns were filed in 1982. In 1985 the number climbed to 17 million. By 1990 it jumped to 20.4 million. And in 1992 it was 21.3 million.
- The percentage of those that were proprietorships—traditionally the structure chosen by fledgling businesses—increased from 69% in 1982 to 71% in 1992.
- Factoring in the growth of the U.S. population, the ratio of entrepreneurs has increased from one out of every 16.2 Americans in 1982 to one out of every 12 in 1992.

Those one out of every 12 Americans realize that the trends that have eliminated workplace security have also paved the road to success for small, start-up companies. Technology now makes it possible for one man working out of his home to do the work that used to require a staff of 10. As global competition forces large companies to focus on their core businesses, small businesses can provide those services and products outside the core. As big companies realize that the size and composition of their staff should correlate directly to their current projects, it opens up opportunities for independent professionals, consultants, and freelancers.

If you want to remain active past the traditional age of retirement, entrepreneurship offers the best hope. In a study of people who have had unusually long careers, author Lydia Brontë found that most started their own businesses in the middle of their careers.

It's also becoming clear that not only is there no security in employment, but there's less risk to entrepreneurship than was once thought. Bruce Phillips of the Small Business Administration and Bruce Kirchoff of the New Jersey Institute of Technology have made waves with their studies that indicate 40% of new companies last at least six years, 30% last at least eight, and only about 18% truly fail (close their doors owing creditors money).

To do justice to this topic would require a series of books rather than a chapter. For our purposes here I'd like first to go over some ideas and concepts I think are essential for you to start your own business successfully. Then I'd like to offer some specific advice about what I think is one of the quickest, least expensive, and most interesting ways of going into business today: starting a mail-order business using the Internet rather than a catalog. There are extensive lists of sources for more information and comprehensive guidance at the back of this book.

Do I Have What It Takes to Succeed as an Entrepreneur?

The true entrepreneur is a personality type that psychologists have spent years studying and writing about. These experts have isolated a series of traits and characteristics common to successful entrepreneurs. While it's not necessary for you to have every one of these traits in order to successfully start your own business, the more you have, the better your chances.

• You're willing to work hard 24 hours a day, seven days a week.

- You're in good health and have an understanding family.
- Status is meaningless to you. If you have to sweep the floor, you'll do it.
- You're supremely self-confident, courageous, and brave.
- You're not a gambler. You prefer moderately risky ventures to long shots. (That's why you're starting a business in an industry you know.)
- You've above average intelligence and a healthy dose of common sense.
- You're excited by challenges and see them as obstacles to be overcome rather than reasons to quit.
- You're committed to excellence in whatever you do.
- You're a realist rather than a dreamer. You set high goals, but they're achievable.
- Creative expression is important to you.
- You've a sense of urgency. You don't know the meaning of the word "procrastination."

What Kinds of Skills Will I Need to Succeed as an Entrepreneur?

If you'll have a staff, a bank account, and customers, you'll need to know how to manage them all. Even if you're going to be working on your own, you'll need to manage time.

Marketing skills and experience will help you identify a niche in the marketplace and who your customer is, as well as how best to reach him.

You'll need the financial savvy to judge and analyze expenses and costs and compare them with revenue and sales.

Sure, these skills can be learned, but it greatly improves your chances of success to start out with technical competence, marketing skills, and financial acumen *in the business you are about to enter.* That means you need to have some experience in the industry you plan on entering. (If you don't, turn to the next chapter.)

How Can I Come up with an Idea for My Own Business?

I believe there are really only three basic ideas behind successful businesses: offer something that addresses an existing need that has previously gone unsatisfied; offer something that addresses an existing need better than any of the alternatives; or offer something that is so revolutionary, it creates its own need. Let's look at each.

Perhaps the most common idea used to start new businesses is to introduce a new product or service that addresses a need of the customer that has previously gone unsatisfied.

Usually the idea comes when the entrepreneur realizes he has a need that isn't being addressed and then figures out how to satisfy it. His satisfaction then is translated into customer satisfaction. The trick here is to make sure there really is an existing need for your idea.

The second idea is to take someone else's original idea and elaborate or improve on it so your product or service is better at answering a customer's existing need. Your improvement could be in design, marketing, durability, cost, location, delivery, production, or any of a hundred different areas.

However, I'd urge you not to pursue lower price as the element that sets you apart. That invites competition, and since you're small, you won't have the economies of scale to compete on price with larger organizations.

The VCR is an example of the third idea: something that creates a need that didn't previously exist. Before there were VCRs I bet you couldn't have come up with a single reason for recording a TV show. Before there were VCRs there weren't any movies out there going unwatched because of lack of equipment. It was only after the VCR was introduced that needs for it developed.

While this third type of idea can be the most profitable, it's almost impossible for a small business to achieve. To create a need you'll have to spend incredible amounts of money on advertising and marketing before you bring in a penny. And I'm assuming you don't have a bottomless pit of cash to draw from.

How Can I Judge Whether My Idea Will Work?

It's only experience in a particular business or industry that lets you be sure a need actually exists, that it isn't being addressed, or that you can address it better than anyone else.

You have to know if people will pay for what you're offering and how much they'll pay. You have to know how much they'll value excellence. You have to know exactly what a particular customer needs and wants.

You don't need to spend a small fortune on market research. Instead put together your own focus group of friends, relatives, and professionals and tell them your idea. Ask for their opinions. Ask your banker what he thinks. Speak to industry contacts whose intelligence you respect and who in turn will respect the confidentiality of what you're telling them. Talk to other entrepreneurs in similar businesses that aren't potential competitors. Above all, don't let your ego get caught up in your idea. Listen to and accept criticism.

Should I Patent My Idea Right Away?

I'm always amazed at the level of paranoia in my clients who are fledgling entrepreneurs. Almost every one of them is worried someone will steal his idea and is obsessed with obtaining patents, trademarks, or copyright protection. While these federally sanctioned protective devices can be valuable, they're also expensive and time-consuming to pursue. I encourage my clients to take steps short of applying for federal protection.

Start a daily diary as soon as you begin thinking of ideas and take notes on your thoughts. Have them signed by someone not directly involved in the business. When you come up with an idea you think you'll pursue, write a brief description of it and have it read, signed, and dated by two people. Simply send a copy of this to the Disclosure Document Program of the Patent and Trademark Office in Washington, D.C. This provides powerful evidence of the date of your idea.

Whom Should I Turn to for Advice?

Entrepreneurs are by nature independent and egotistical. They don't think anyone can or will do something as well as themselves. But if you want to succeed in business, you're going to have to temper this trait and put together a team of lawyers, accountants, architects, insurance brokers, and real estate specialists to help you navigate areas where you don't have expertise. Go without professional help and you'll spend so much time doing, you'll have no time for thinking.

The best way to find good professionals is through personal recommendation from someone who's in a similar business. Interview each candidate. Look for someone with commercial experience. Make sure the terms of your relationship—including fees—are spelled out in an engagement letter.

How Big a Target Market Should I Aim For?

Any product or service for sale, no matter how innovative or extraordinary, must be targeted at both a market and a customer. And the narrower, more precise the targeting, the better.

Customers are individuals or businesses that have both the desire and financial resources to purchase your product or service.

Markets are groups of customers.

Since no one business can answer the needs of every customer in a market, you need to focus your efforts on a segment of the market. Markets can be divided, or segmented, by demographics, benefits, or rate of use.

Demographic segmentation categorizes customers by geographic, social, or economic factors. Combine factors and you come up with a composite customer—for instance, young, single, upper-income women.

Benefit segmentation categorizes customers by the reason they purchase a product or service. Examples would be appearance or value.

Rate of use segmentation breaks down a market according to how frequently someone uses the service or buys the product. Examples would be frequent users, occasional users, and nonusers.

The market segment you target should be reflected in every aspect of your business from its location to its marketing.

How Can I Estimate What My Sales and Market Share Will Be?

Determine the size of the industry you're about to enter. Then figure out the size of the market segment you're targeting. Use census data to come up with numbers on consumers and the Yellow Pages to come up with numbers on businesses. Be conservative in your numbers.

Try to figure out the market shares of the existing players in the business. Use financial reports, Dun & Bradstreet reports, and any other sources you can find. Estimate how you'll do in comparison with those existing businesses. Be realistic, not pessimistic or optimistic.

Use these conservative and realistic estimates to come up with your projected sales figures.

Is Location Still the Key to Success?

People used to say the three keys to success in business were location, location, and location. Today you'd be more accurate saying there's one key: access.

What you can do and what you can offer are more important

to the customer today than where you are. What matters most is how accessible you are.

Information and communication is flowing over the international telecommunications web 24 hours a day, seven days a week. The world may not be shrinking physically, but the ability of customers to reach across the miles to buy products and services has made it a smaller place for business owners.

With accessibility and the technology to take advantage of it, you can reach into new markets and become a more forceful competitor. If you're good at what you do, you can look beyond commuting distance when trying to market your service. If your product is good, you can reach beyond the limited numbers of people who can physically visit a storefront.

Using fax machines, modems, videoconferencing, E-mail, printed catalogs, and electronic catalogs on the World Wide Web, your service or retail business can reach a global audience while remaining located in your home office and while keeping your inventory in your garage or basement. Depending on your business, an exciting page on the World Wide Web could be more important than a prestigious mailing address or storefront location.

Not only does focusing on access rather than location allow you to expand your potential audience, but it can cut your start-up and operating costs dramatically.

Buying cutting-edge technology for a home-based retail or service operation will cost much less than setting up an office or store. And the upkeep and maintenance costs will be far less than the rent you'd pay.

Sure, you have to be certain your product or service will allow for this kind of home-based electronic-oriented business. But if it does, I think you'd be foolish not to choose this more modern, more exciting, and less costly approach.

But What Should I Look for If I Want to Open a Traditional Retail Store?

Stand-alone buildings offer excellent access, visibility, and control over the immediate environment and allow for expansion. However, they offer little traffic and, therefore, little chance for impulse shopping.

Small strip shopping centers attract customers interested in fast service.

Community shopping centers draw more impulse buyers but are also more expensive.

Large regional shopping centers are the most expensive and draw primarily browsing shoppers.

Neighboring stores have a powerful effect on the success of your location. A shoe salon will do better located next to a clothing store than a hardware store. Some businesses do better surrounded by other, similar stores—restaurants, for example—while others fare better when the competition isn't close by—drugstores, for instance.

Make sure to check on visibility. If no one can see your signage, it doesn't matter if thousands pass by each day.

Check parking availability. If you're relying on people to drive to your location, try parking your own car nearby. People will go someplace else if they can't park quickly and easily.

A main road with a center mall or median impeding left-hand turns will generate only as much traffic as a one-way street. If traffic moves so fast that slowing down, turning, or parking is dangerous, you'll lose any advantage from being on a main road.

Corner locations draw traffic from both cross streets, doubling walk-in trade.

Locations near subway and bus stops offer an extra surge in walk-in, convenience-oriented customers.

In the winter there will be more foot traffic on the sunny side of the street—in the summer it will be the opposite.

Aren't All Commercial Leases Standardized Documents?

Not only are all leases negotiable, but they must be amended if you're to succeed in business. Ask your attorney to examine any proposed lease. You and she should make sure to address the following points:

- Get a short lease with options to renew that extend at least as far as your anticipated break-even point.
- Sign as a corporation, not an individual, to insulate against personal liability.
- Make sure the lease accurately reflects the square footage of the space.
- Examine very carefully the charges for such things as lobby areas, air-conditioning, heating, taxes, and insurance.
- Make sure the lease is assignable and that the location can be used for "any legal use."
- Pay close attention to any rights the landlord has to cancel the lease.
- Make sure rent increases are described, both in amount and timing.
- An occupancy date should be stated. If the space isn't delivered as promised by that date, you should have the right to terminate the agreement.

What About Technology? What Should Be My Primary Concern?

Time is the one resource an entrepreneur has no way of storing or replenishing. You're going to be constantly challenged to make productive use of your every working moment. That's why telecommunications technology should be your primary concern.

With a fax machine or a modem-equipped computer your bid can be in your client's office as soon as it's completed. You can carry a portable telephone with you, wherever you go. If you leave information you need at your office, you can connect with your desk computer from your laptop by modem and retrieve the data you need. When you're away or on the telephone, an answering machine, voice mail, or electronic mail system can receive your messages. Incoming messages can be transmitted directly to an alphanumeric pocket pager carried with you.

But just because the technology exists doesn't mean it's worth buying. In order to figure that out, ask yourself the following questions about whatever tool or service you're considering:

- Will it let you use your time more productively?
- Will it enable you to do a better job of what you're already doing?
- Will it help you broaden your reach in the marketplace?
- Will it improve your customer service by reducing response time or giving clients better access to you?
- Will it eventually pay for itself in cost savings, increased productivity, or expanded sales opportunities?

It's easy to lose sight of what you *need* to accomplish in the excitement generated by new technology. The bottom line is that technology should improve how you already work. Invest in tools for which you have a proven use. Then expand as your needs evolve.

Finally, make sure you realize that technology can make you accessible 24 hours a day—if that's what you want. You must decide how accessible you want to be and respect that schedule. Technology should help you make more productive use of your day, not turn you into a slave.

Obviously I'll Need a Computer, Too. . . . What Kind Should I Buy?

Buying a computer system for your new business can seem a daunting task. You can make it much simpler by watching out for some common mistakes.

Too many entrepreneurs buy their hardware first. That's putting the cart before the horse. Decide which software meets your needs, then choose the hardware that runs it.

When comparing prices, make sure you're comparing apples to apples. The price of one system might seem higher, but when the cost of its extra features are considered, it may be a better deal.

Usually bundles of software that come along with hardware purchases are a good deal, but be careful. Check the retail prices of the programs and make sure they're applications you'll use.

You can't have enough RAM (random access memory).

Don't get caught up in the promise of the technology of tomorrow. For most entrepreneurs, the more reasonably priced technology of today will be sufficient for your needs.

When in doubt, buy the system that will be easier for you to use. Your computer can offer gains in productivity and accuracy only if you use it!

Screens that can portray millions of colors sound wonderful, but most entrepreneurs need only two colors: black and white. Contrast and clarity are more important than colors unless you're in a business that depends on colors, such as graphics or fashion.

Make sure to read the fine print in mail-order computer ads before you buy. Watch out for terms such as "restocking fee" and "cash price." They actually mean "nonrefundable" and "real prices are higher." And "factory recertified" is often another way of saying "used."

What's the Best Way to Market My New Business?

Despite all the attention paid to advertising and public relations, I think the key marketing efforts for a beginning entrepreneur are those that convey his image.

- Since your face and smile can't be everywhere, you need a logo that sends the same message as you. Your logo should be on your stationery, on shopping bags . . . everywhere it will fit. If it's unique, fun, intelligent, or intriguing, all the better.

- Signs aren't going to bring herds of new customers to your store, but they can have a cumulative, almost subliminal effectiveness. Using banners along with signs will give you more exposure.
- The message on your answering machine should be businesslike, without music and jokes. The telephone should be answered promptly and politely.
- You and your staff should be nonthreatening and pleasant in manner, neat, clean, and businesslike in appearance.
- Make sure your office or store is well lit, sparkling clean, and inviting. Have fresh flowers around—they add charm and cover odors.
- Products on display should look clean and fresh.
- Your window displays should be invitations for people to enter, whether you're a retailer or a service provider. You're paying a premium for storefront space, so you might as well use it to your advantage.
- Decide what sets your business apart, then articulate it and communicate it through as many avenues as you can so your customers start to remember it.
- Set yourself up as an expert. Daily newspapers and industry trade reporters are always on the lookout for new sources for stories and comments.
- Create your own mailing list of business contacts—prospects, suppliers, customers, investors, etc.—and send information to them regularly.
- Support local charities and causes by donating your products or your time.

Should I Set My Prices Simply by Marking up My Costs or by Seeing What My Competitors Are Charging?

Most fledgling entrepreneurs fail to realize that their pricing strategy is an important part of their overall marketing effort.

Setting a price close to a competitor's price works only when both firms are established. Such comparable pricing doesn't give your competitor's customers any reason to switch to you.

The best option for a new small business is actually to set prices higher than the competition and back them up with an image of quality. This not only sets you apart from the competition, but it helps recover start-up costs quickly.

If you're selling products, consider good-better-best pricing. This gives customers choices within the same product line. One offers the best price, one the best value, and one the best quality.

Remember, the key is to start high. You can always drop a price and win customers. It's far more difficult to raise a price and keep them.

Where Can I Get My Seed Money?

The best place, obviously, is from your own personal savings. If the business you're starting is fairly modest—say, a home-based consulting firm—it's entirely possible to fund it with the money you've been setting aside for a rainy day, your retirement, or junior's Harvard tuition.

Of course, raiding your savings in this way means risking your family's future and security. However, that's a risk many if not most entrepreneurs have to take if they want to get started in business. They have the confidence that their business will succeed and they'll eventually be able to pay back the funds they've raided—and then put away even more.

Raiding designated tax-deferred retirement plans, such as IRAs, SEPs and 401(k)s, has tax ramifications as well. Before you pull any funds out of these kinds of accounts, speak with your tax adviser.

Borrowing Your Seed Money

If you don't have any savings to draw on, the next option is to borrow the money. But no financial institution will loan money to a start-up business, period. They *will* loan money to an entrepreneur personally, however. That means that in order to borrow money for your business you'll need to take out either a personal loan based on your credit or a home-equity loan using your house as collateral.

Taking out a personal loan is just one shade better than funding the business with credit cards. The amount of money you can borrow will be limited and the interest rates will be quite high, putting tremendous pressure on the business from day one. People have successfully launched businesses with money from personal loans, but they're few and far between.

A better option is to borrow against the equity you have in your house. Assuming you own your home and have built up equity in it, you could borrow a considerable amount of money. The interest you'd be paying on this kind of loan would be comparatively low. In addition, it's apt to be tax-deductible.

Of course, taking out a home-equity loan carries some risks. You are gambling the roof over your head (and the heads of your family members) on the success of your business. Once again, it's a risk you may need to take if you're going to succeed as an entrepreneur.

How Do I Approach Family and Friends for Money?

Another alternative is to borrow money from friends and relatives. This actually goes hand in hand with investing your own savings since no one—not even your beloved aunt Tilly—is going to lend you money unless you've already invested your own funds.

It's important to realize that borrowing from family and

friends is not the same as asking for charity. You're an entrepreneur offering an investment opportunity. They may also get some tax advantages and a share of future profits after your business turns successful.

Treat this exchange like a business deal. Think carefully about whom to approach. Identify all the people you know. Eliminate those who might question your decision making, worry about the risk you're taking, or cause trouble if your business were to fail. Ask whoever is left for an agreement that they won't interfere in the management of your business.

Have a business plan ready, as well as a funding proposal, describing how much you need, how you'll use it, whether you'll ask for more later, the terms by which you'll repay the investment, and how they'll share in your profits.

Ask for loans at the prevailing interest rate or perhaps a little below, and trade ownership (in the corporation in the form of shares of common stock) for an investment of equity capital. Your accountant or attorney can help you set a value on the stock.

How you present your proposal will depend on your relationship to the potential investor, but keep these general rules in mind:

- Break the ice by saying something like "I've come to you for a combination of advice and help. I have some good news: I have been saving money, studying the market, waiting for the right moment to go into business for myself, and the time has come."
- If your potential investor voices an objection, answer it. For example, if he says "I'm not the one to help you," you might say "I think you are. You're one of the most business-savvy people I know."
- Next, present your business plan.
- If another objection is expressed, again, acknowledge it and turn it into a positive answer. For example, if he says "That kind of business sounds like a big gamble," you might say "That's true sometimes, but let me show you how mine would work."

- Then present your financing proposal.
- After this, answer any remaining concerns and, as in every sales effort, ask for a commitment.

The obvious downside to going to family and friends for start-up funds is that you're mixing your business and personal lives. You'll have to accept that your relationship with your lenders/investors will be changed as long as they're involved in your business. It's unrealistic to expect your relationship with your brother-in-law to stay the same if you borrow $5,000 from him. Until you pay it back, with the promised interest, things will be different.

Taking on a Partner

You may be lucky enough to have a friend or relative who's in the position to become a partner in your business. Perhaps he has sufficient money to put up a percentage of the seed money needed in return for part ownership of the business and a percentage of the annual profits. It could be a very lucrative investment.

The way partners decide to operate a business determines how profits are shared. If your partner is involved in another business, he can be a silent partner and let you be responsible for running the operation.

Let's say you have a brother-in-law who is a successful stock options trader. You and he both could put up half the money needed to start the business, say, $15,000 each. While you each own half the business, since you're the one running the business day to day, you agree that you'll get 80% of the operating profits.

The first year, the business nets $10,000. Your portion is $8,000, and your brother-in-law's would be $2,000. That's a great return on his $15,000 investment. If the business performs well and is eventually sold, half the profit would be his.

There are many other ways partnerships can be set up. Each

has different legal considerations and requires the expertise of an attorney experienced in business partnerships.

There are, of course, downsides to partnerships. Two heads aren't always better than one. If both heads have different ideas about how things should be handled, the business can go down the tubes while the partners are fighting it out. That's why it's crucial that the responsibilities and authority of all the partners be defined in a partnership agreement. That's also why I encourage my clients to pursue silent, rather than active, partners.

What Should I Do about a Salary for Myself?

One of the biggest mistakes fledgling entrepreneurs make is not providing for themselves adequately during the start-up phase of the business. There are two ways you can do this: establish a financial cushion before you open the business, or factor a salary into your financial projections from day one.

Ideally a financial cushion should be enough money to cover 18 months of your personal expenses, above and beyond the money you need to start the business. After six months you'll have a good idea of whether or not the business will make it. But it could take another year after that for the business to become profitable enough for you to draw a salary.

The other option is to factor in an acceptable, livable salary for yourself from day one. The only problem with this is that entrepreneurs have a tendency to first cut their own salary in response to any business problems.

Do I Need to Prepare a Business Plan
Even If I'm Not Borrowing Money?

While most people think the primary purpose of a business plan is to have something to show potential investors and lenders, I'm of the opinion that its most valuable role is as a map for your business effort. A business plan can take you from inception to success and even predict your failure.

Drawing up a business plan will force you to think logically, to examine potential problems, and to make realistic assessments of your future earnings. It will force you to question your assumptions and ideas every step along the way.

With a business plan you'll be able to judge your progress. You'll know when you should break even and when you should start turning a profit. You'll know how much sales volume you need to generate in order to stay afloat. A business plan lets you establish minimum standards so you know if you're on the road to riches or a going-out-of-business sale.

I know what you're thinking. Your operation is going to be small. There's no need to go to all this trouble. Besides, none of the entrepreneurs you know drafted a business plan until they had to go out and get a bank loan. I too know entrepreneurs who succeeded without a formal written business plan. But for every one of them who succeeded without a business plan there are hundreds who failed because they lacked a logical, formal plan of attack.

A business plan, drawn up before you open your doors and updated regularly, will be important as a means of checking your operation's health. If you know how much seed financing you need to start, how much operating capital you need to keep open, and how much revenue you need to bring in, you'll be able to set minimum goals. Fall below them and you're going to fail. The sooner you realize that, the less money you'll lose.

How Should I Structure My Business?

The vast majority of entrepreneurs structure their businesses as sole proprietorships. That's because it's the simplest business structure and the cheapest to set up. Basically you and the business are the same. That certainly makes filing taxes and keeping records simple. However, there's a risk to this simplicity. Since you and the business are the same, its liabilities are yours. If the business gets sued, your personal assets can be attacked. If you were a corporation, on the other hand, only the assets of the corporation could be attacked.

Sure, corporations are more complex and expensive to set up and may cost you a bit more in taxes. But I think they're well worth the added costs. As soon as you can, speak to your accountant and attorney about setting up what's called an S corporation. That's a very simple corporation form that, while almost as simple as a sole proprietorship, offers a great deal more protection from liability.

How Do I Find Good Employees?

It's not too tough to determine a job candidate's technical expertise: check his résumé and his references. But that's not usually why employees fail. They generally become problems because they can't work as part of a team, they're not flexible, or their expectations haven't been met. Good interviewing can help you spot potential problem employees before you hire them. Here are some questions to ask:

- Describe an instance where you used an atypical solution to solve a typical problem. His answer will demonstrate his creativity.
- What do you believe is the personal profile for someone to be successful at this job? His answer will demonstrate if his expectations match the job description.
- Describe a situation in which you were a member of a team but disagreed with the way others wanted to approach a project. His answer will demonstrate his teamwork skills.
- What do you consider a positive work environment? His answer will show whether or not he will be comfortable in your environment.
- Describe the best/worst boss you ever had. His answer will demonstrate his expectations on how he should be managed.
- How would you define success in life? His answer will demonstrate his personal and professional priorities, values, sense of life balance, motivation, and maturity.

Whenever possible during an interview, keep your mouth shut. Try to talk only 20% of the time and listen 80% of the time. You'll learn more about the candidate that way.

What's the Key Thing I Should Watch for Once I'm up and Running?

Without cash on hand your business will die, regardless of how high its sales are or how profitable it is on paper. Cash flow is the difference between what you take in and what you pay out. If a business pays out more than it takes in, it will, obviously, be short of cash.

Cash won't necessarily come in when a customer makes a purchase or go out when you place an order. Few businesses are run on a totally cash-and-carry basis. Most of your customers and clients will want to pay for goods or services some time after they've actually acquired them. And you will want to pay your suppliers, staff, and creditors some time after you acquire goods or services from them. The trick, obviously, is to get the cash from your customers or clients before you have to pay your own bills.

In order to do that you'll need to be able to forecast and analyze the cash flow of your business. You'll need to know when a big bill is coming in and when sales are going to slow down. The sooner you can predict problems, the more time you'll have to solve them. You don't want to close shop on Friday and suddenly realize you won't be able to pay your bills on Monday.

Project your income month by month. Subtract from each month's income what it will cost you to keep the business up and running. Obviously these numbers will be estimates in the beginning, but over time you'll replace them with actual numbers. Your projections will have to be based on a series of assumptions about your sales, customer payment terms, supplier payment terms, loan or investment payback terms, and any reinvestment of cash into the business. Work forward at least until you can show the business breaking even.

In order to continue using cash flows to gauge the health of your businesses, you'll need to keep accurate records of all of your finances. If you do nothing else with a computer system, the ability to easily compute and analyze cash flows makes it a worthwhile purchase.

How Can I Improve Cash Flow?

One way of maximizing your cash flow is to speed up the accounts receivable process. If you were to alter your payment terms from the standard 30 days to 15 days—or less—it could substantially lessen your need to borrow money and increase cash flow.

Make sure you invoice immediately. Too many fledgling entrepreneurs wait to send out their bills, guaranteeing a slow-down in the payment cycle.

Similarly, begin your collection efforts the day after payments are due. This shows you're concerned about getting paid on time and will probably result in your getting paid ahead of the rest of the pack.

Start your collection effort with a friendly reminder. If the first reminder fails to yield payment, send another copy of the invoice, along with a cover letter stating you thought it important to put in writing your understanding of the situation to date. Most customers will respond to the implied threat.

Try to negotiate longer payment terms on your accounts payable. Find out if your vendors will accept payment within 60 days rather than the standard 30.

Many entrepreneurs are afraid to ask for faster payment and for more time to pay their own bills, for fear of alienating customers and suppliers. I've found that few customers are likely to balk and that a surprising number of suppliers are willing to be more flexible.

What Kinds of Records Should I Keep?

As soon as you become self-employed your chances of being audited by the IRS increase dramatically. That's because the IRS considers self-employed taxpayers easy targets since so many fail to keep adequate documentation. To stay one step ahead of the revenue agents you must be well organized and prepared to substantiate every item you report or declare. The burden of proof is on you, the taxpayer.

Realize that if the deductions you report are large in proportion to your income, or you report an overall business loss for several years running, you're just about inviting an IRS inquiry. Large deductions for business meals and entertainment are always problems, too. Also, if you forget to file certain required forms, you'll at least trigger some correspondence. However, if you follow a few simple steps, you should steer clear of trouble.

- Keep a separate bank account used exclusively for your business, and keep a monthly reconciliation of all your cash receipts and disbursements with the bank statement.
- Maintain a "paid bill" file, organized in alphabetical order, which contains all your tax-deductible expenses for the year.
- Keep a separate file with copies of all the invoices of the fixed assets used in your business (computer, fax machine) on which you are claiming a tax deduction for depreciation.
- If you're deducting expenses for business meals, remember to keep records of the four *w*'s: *Where* and *when* did the meal take place? *Whom* did you dine with and *what* was the item of business you discussed? Don't forget that business meals are only 50% deductible for tax purposes.
- If you're deducting expenses for a home office, be prepared to show that the office is used exclusively as your principal place of business, where you meet regularly with clients. A separate telephone line is a must for those working from home.
- You're required to keep records of your business mileage, showing odometer readings if you're taking deductions for the

business use of an automobile. Also, your business trips should be described in your business diary or calendar.

• Keep records of your business income and deductions for at least six years after you file your return—in certain circumstances the IRS can go back that far in an audit.

Are There Any "Secrets" to Success in Business?

Obviously, having read this far, you know there are no shortcuts to success in your own business. I've offered some tips and advice to help smooth the way, and you'll find more detailed advice in the sources I'll suggest in a minute. But before you turn to those, I just wanted to share with you some of the philosophies I've picked up in more than three decades of advising entrepreneurs and being one myself.

TRADITIONAL VALUES PAY OFF

Care for your staff, your clients, and even your suppliers and landlord. Treat others as you'd like to be treated. Work hard to give 110% effort at everything you do. Offer help to those who need it. Be honest.

LOOK FORWARD TO THE FUTURE

To be a successful entrepreneur you have to wake up enthusiastic, greet the dawn with joy, see the wonder of life, view problems as just obstacles to overcome.

EXPERIENCE IS VITAL

How can you know what will work unless you have firsthand knowledge of the industry? How can you work out marketing plans when you have no idea of what has or hasn't worked for others? How can you buy and stock a healthy inventory without first seeing how others have done it?

BRING THE CUSTOMER TO YOU

Don't think that people will beat a path to your door just because you've opened it. Sure, some will. But not enough for you to be successful. Get out there and bring them to your business.

START EARLY AND STOP LATE

The more time you spend on the business, the more successful you'll be. Remember, you pay rent for 24 hours. Why not use as many of them as you can for business? Eat, breathe, and sleep business. You won't mind it if you love what you're doing—in fact, it will be fun.

UNDERSTAND THE POWER OF SILENCE

If you don't know the answer to a question—say so, then offer to find out. If you have nothing to say—say nothing.

LOVE WHAT YOU'RE DOING

The mere fact of starting your own business should be enough to make you love it. The business may not be your spouse, but it is one of your children. Treat it that way.

RESPECT YOUR STAFF

A happy place of business does well. Treat your staff well. Make them feel that they are participants. Say "we" instead of "I." No one objects to structure, as long as it is fair and based on respect.

YOU CAN'T DO IT ALONE

No man is an island. Reach out to others for help and advice. That's a sign of intelligence and humility, not stupidity and weakness. Take your professionals into your confidence. Treat friends and family as valued team members. Ask for advice and listen to what they have to say.

WHEN IN DOUBT, DO IT

Don't hesitate or procrastinate. Both are deadly to small businesses. While you're wasting time, others are taking action, beating you to the punch. No mistake is so large that it can't be corrected.

HAVE A LIST OF POLICIES

Is the customer always right? Will you always accept merchandise returned, whatever the reason? Have a policy for every set of major circumstances. As new situations arise, create new policies to address them.

SIGNAL GOOD MANAGEMENT

Exude knowledge. Know your numbers and industry inside out. Let the information come out of your pores. Study it so hard that it becomes ingrained on your brain. You never have to demonstrate knowledge—it will come out of its own accord.

USE THE SHORTCUT TO CREATING TRUST

Most business transactions are too short to actually create trust. Instead show the other party you care about them.

GET OUT OF YOUR OWN WAY

We do things to ourselves we would never let others do to us. Stop worrying about the repercussions of every action you take and just start working. You'll find that when you're busy you aren't worried. Concentrate on the rowing and let fate do the steering.

ACT AS IF EVERY DAY WERE OPENING DAY

Competition is out there, just waiting for you to sit back and rest on your laurels. Never stop thinking up new ideas, looking for original approaches, or formulating new directions. All businesses are heading toward either success or failure—there is no middle ground.

The Internet: Shortcut to Entrepreneurial Success

The Internet isn't going to revolutionize business . . . it already has. Thousands of companies, large and small, are already on-line. And thousands more are going online every day. As of the end of 1995 there were more than 150,000 commercial sites on the Internet and another 2,000 being added each week, according to InterNIC, an organization that maintains Internet addresses.

Some of these businesses are using the Internet as little more than an electronic billboard, offering a simple description of a product or service and a way to obtain further information. But others are providing the equivalent of a comprehensive, even interactive, catalog with the capability of taking orders on-line. In effect, they're creating virtual storefronts or cyberstores. What's more interesting is that the majority of those companies offering such virtual storefronts are small businesses.

It could cost millions for a large retailer to create a suitable presence on the Internet. For instance, think of how much time, effort, and money would have to go into putting the Montgomery Ward catalog on-line. A small, specialized company, however, could create and service an extraordinary presence for less than $10,000.

What Makes Doing Business on the Internet So Attractive?

For starters, it's a big market. Estimates are there are somewhere between 25 and 30 million people connected to the Internet.

And by and large, these people are attractive customers. According to surveys and studies by A. C. Nielsen, Internet users are younger and more highly educated than the average American, with higher than average incomes. They shop and spend more than average at office supply stores, electronics stores, bookstores, department stores, home improvement stores, and music stores. They read and use mail-order catalogs more often. They spend more on baby food, diapers, and other baby needs than average and spend more than most in specialty pet stores. In other words, they're young, affluent people who either have children or treat their pets like children. That's a very attractive customer profile for many businesses.

For these attractive customers, E-mail ordering is even easier than telephone or fax ordering. There are no busy signals. There's no being put on hold, waiting for someone to take your order. And there are no times when the business is closed. Orders can be solicited and taken 24 hours a day, seven days a week, 52 weeks a year.

It's easy to run a cyberstore by yourself, eliminating the costs and headaches of employees. You don't have to be present for your store to be open, so unlike real retailers, you won't have to put in extremely long, inconvenient hours.

Finally, setting up a virtual storefront on the Internet can be easy and affordable.

How Do I Create a Web Site?

There are today many Web service businesses that will design your page and obtain a URL (uniform resource locator, or Web address) and an E-mail address for you. Many of these shops offer graphic design services as well. The cost of designing a Web page will depend on the complexity and size of the site. You can also work out a consulting arrangement with these designers so they'll help with regular updating, upgrading, and problem solving. Of course, if you want to learn HTML (hypertext markup language, the basic tool for formatting text on a Web page), you could do it yourself.

Aside from this start-up cost you'll have to pay for a regular Internet connection. That could be as little as $20 a month if you use a local Internet service provider (ISP). This same ISP can keep your site on their computer and act as its "server." The fee for this will also depend on the complexity of your site. You could use your own computer to serve the site, but be forewarned: it can take a great deal of memory to service an attractive site around the clock. And if you're not going to be open around the clock, you're losing out on one of the major benefits of being on-line. If you work with an ISP, all you'll need is a run-of-the-mill computer that will let you receive and respond to your E-mail orders and do the rest of the business functions you require.

Is E-Mail Safe for Financial Transactions?

Concerns about the security of credit card numbers as they move around cyberspace are legitimate. Of course, credit card numbers moving over telephone lines (by voice or fax) are just as insecure; it's just that the insecurity isn't so publicized. However, security fears are being addressed by the movers and shakers of the computer industry. Early in 1996 Microsoft Corporation and Netscape Communications announced their intention to develop an industry-standard technology to protect the security of credit card transactions in cyberspace. By the time you read this book it's likely the new standard will be in effect.

How Does a Customer Find a "Cyberstore"?

Most people find sites on the Internet by using a "search engine"—a program that, using a keyword or -words, finds the names and URLs of sites that match the keyword. That's yet another reason it makes sense to have a pro put together and name your URL. Among the most popular search engines are Infoseek, Magellan, Excite, Lycos, Alta Vista, and Yahoo.

Another way sites are found is by following "links." These are like "hot" buttons on a site; when pressed by someone, they instantly connect the user to another site. Many complementary (but not competitive) Web merchants create "links" to each other. Techno-savvy regular customers of yours could put links on their own personal Web pages that connect to your site. You might even offer discounts for such a service, since the more links you have to your site, the more potential customers you'll have stopping by your cyberstore.

Of course, customers can also respond to regular advertisements that promote your site. Remember, people who spend time on the Internet still read newspapers and magazines.

How Much Does It Cost to Start and Run a "Cyberstore"?

The answer to this question is what ultimately makes doing business on the Internet extremely attractive.

If you run your cyberstore from your home, your overhead could be limited to monthly charges for your regular advertising, your Internet service, the dedicated telephone line for your modem, shipping charges, inventory replenishment, and your electric bill. Your start-up costs could consist solely of computer and office equipment, Web page design fees, office supplies, your initial inventory, and any start-up advertising you do. Arguably you could be up and running a store in your spare time for less than $10,000. That's about as cheap a way to go into business as I've ever seen.

What Kinds of Cyberstores Have the Best Chance for Success?

Based on the demographics of the customer base and the impersonal nature of the relationship between merchant and customer, your best bet for success as a cybermerchant is to run a highly specialized product business—for instance, a business that sells CDs and tapes of music from Central and South America; a store that peddles left-handed tools; or a site that promotes products for people who own a particular breed of dog. Service businesses could use the Internet for marketing, but it's doubtful anyone would establish a business relationship based solely on cybercontact—face-to-face meetings are still pretty much the rule in the service business.

The Story of Emily Krakow

Emily Krakow has been my client for a long time. She and her husband, Peter, first came to see me when they moved to New York City in 1982 and were looking for a lawyer to help them negotiate the purchase of an apartment. A few years later I helped Emily work out strategies to get a raise from the national bookstore chain she worked for. And when they were expecting their first child, I helped Emily and Peter reorganize and plan their personal finances.

About 18 months ago Emily came to see me yet again. This time it was about her career. She'd climbed the ladder to become manager of a very large chain bookstore—one of New York's biggest "superbookstores." In order to move further in the company she'd have to be willing to relocate and move into the corporate rather than retail end of the business. She wasn't interested in either possibility, and besides, she was feeling very frustrated at the restraints the corporation put on her ideas.

The company was still concerned with mass appeal and marketing, while Emily was beginning to see the shortcomings inherent in the superstore concept. She wanted to do more niche marketing and cultivate individual relationships with customers, albeit with lots of customers at the same time. She proposed compiling an exhaustive database that, when coupled with the store's own desktop publishing system, could generate what amounted to personalized newsletters. If, for instance, the database showed a particular customer routinely bought books on cooking and history, his newsletter would contain a listing of the latest offerings in those two categories, along with relevant reviews, tips, and articles. While her regional director thought the idea had merit, the national headquarters wouldn't let her pull staffers off the floor to prepare the program and wouldn't give her the additional funds to hire new people.

Peter was doing very well in his job as comptroller for a major clothing manufacturer. Together their income was nearly $150,000. After going over their finances and hearing Emily's frustration, Peter suggested they could absorb a cut in her income, especially if it was temporary and resulted in her being happier.

That's when they came to me. I listened to both of them. We all went through the exercises outlined earlier in this book. The more we talked about it, the clearer it became that Emily should give entrepreneurship a shot. After a few sessions together, the three of us developed a plan for Emily to open her own business.

The plan called for it to start as a simple mail-order catalog for specialized cookbooks—the one particular niche Emily thought had the greatest potential and wasn't being adequately addressed by the superstores. The entire operation would be run out of her apartment, since she was able to get distributors to ship books directly to her customers, through a process called "drop shipping." Emily would concentrate her advertising efforts on display classified ads in upscale cooking magazines and a very professionally designed Web page on the World Wide Web. Rather than putting out an annual catalog, she'd send a free newsletter to customers that mirrored the type of brochure she'd suggested to her boss. Satisfied with the plan, they started getting their funds together.

They both began cutting back on their discretionary spending. They didn't take a vacation. They stopped eating out altogether. They gave up movies and the theater, concentrating on television and videos for entertainment. They didn't rent a summer cottage, instead spending lots of time at local parks and pools. They upped their insurance deductibles. After six months they had banked about $15,000, close to what they needed for their start-up costs. In order to cover their operating costs for the 18 months we'd figured it would take for the business to start making money, they took out a home-equity line of credit. From the beginning we'd factored in a salary for Emily that, while almost $30,000 less than she was currently earning, would be sufficient for them to get by.

Almost a year to the day after they came into my office, Emily launched the Complete Gourmet Book Service. In the past six months the business has become so successful that she's thinking of expanding and starting a second catalog for specialized children's books. She's excited by the constant challenges and the opportunities to express her creativity. She's never been happier. And despite the change in their lifestyle, they both say they'd do it again in a minute.

For More Information

For sources of more information and advice on starting your own business, see Appendix Two on page 203.

CHAPTER 10

Start Your Own Business in a Different Industry

THE FACTS AT A GLANCE

- Feasibility: 1
- Risk: 5+ if you start an original business, 5 if you buy a franchise or an existing business
- Problems it **will** solve: not rewarding emotionally, maxed out in company, maxed out in industry, no longer challenging, unhealthy environment
- Time: 9 to 12 months for an original business, 6 to 9 months if you buy a franchise or an existing business

---

Before you go any further, turn back to Chapter 9 and read about starting a business in the same industry you're in now. Why? Because in all good conscience I cannot recommend you start a business in an industry in which you've no experience. As you'll learn in Chapter 9, one of the most important elements in being a successful entrepreneur is to have experience in the business. So if you've chosen this option, all the advice I'm going to offer centers around ways to compensate for your lack of experience.

Obviously the first way is to forget about starting a business in an industry you know nothing about and stick with what you know. I can only assume you've nixed that idea because you hate your industry with a passion; it's a hatred so fierce that you're willing to take a huge risk to get out of it. But coupled with that hatred is an entrepreneurial spark, an urge to be your own boss.

Okay, there are two general ways you can make up for the fatal gap in your knowledge and successfully start a business in an industry you're not experienced with.

First, you can go back to school and study the industry you're about to enter, while working part-time in the business. In effect you can make up for your lack of experience with an education. If that sounds like an approach you'd be interested in, turn to Chapter 11. Of course, be prepared to take quite a financial hit for a while.

Second, you can buy experience. There are two ways of doing this. You can either purchase an existing business and keep the previous owner around long enough to school you, or you can buy a franchise and take advantage of your franchisor's experience in the business. These are the two options I'll explore in this chapter. Be aware, however, that neither offers all the creativity and control you'd get from starting an original business. However, I think that's a small enough price to pay for making success in this option possible rather than almost impossible.

As in previous chapters, rather than trying to compress a book's (in this case two books') worth of information into a chapter, I'll offer tips, advice, and guidance and then at the back of the book suggest comprehensive resources for you.

Buying an Existing Business

Buying an existing business is intrinsically less risky than starting a business from scratch. You'll realize profits quickly and get a faster return on your initial investments of time and money. An existing business has a track record. It has a location, equipment, inventory, customer base, and staff. A single financial transaction lets you step into the shoes of the owner.

If you're looking to enter an industry in which you have no experience, buying an existing business has the added advantage of providing a built-in teacher: the previous owner. If his continued presence and assistance are made part of the deal, you'll theoretically be able to profit from the business while you're learning it.

Buying an existing business isn't a risk-free proposition, however. It's as easy to inherit ill will as goodwill. The current staff may be incompetent or unmanageable. The equipment may need to be modernized. The inventory could be obsolete. The location could be too expensive or inadequate for expansion.

Finally, it's possible your built-in teacher could be a burned-out malcontent, incapable of passing along knowledge, who couldn't care less whether you or the business last one day longer than it takes for him to cash his final check.

In order to maximize the advantages and minimize or avoid the potential disadvantages, you're going to have to work just as hard as if you were starting your own business from scratch.

How Do I Decide What Business to Buy?

First, forget about buying a business that's up for sale. I know that sounds crazy, but let me explain.

Someone selling a business is selling for a reason. Sure, there are business owners who are actually selling because of illness or retirement. And there are businesses whose owner died and are now being shopped around by an estate. There are also four-leaf clovers. And I'd no more encourage you to look for the first two than I would the third.

More likely a business is up for sale because there's something wrong with it. What's worse, whatever is wrong with it will be obscured. Nothing will necessarily be as it seems. Unless you have enough experience in a business to make an intelligent analysis, you can be taken to the cleaners. And since you're looking at businesses in an industry in which you've no experience, you're almost guaranteed to not only get taken to the cleaners, but to lose your shirt.

Someone who has experience in an industry may be able to look at a business that's up for sale, figure out what's wrong, and come up with ways to correct the problems and turn the place around. But since you've no experience you're simply going to be buying someone else's headache. It would be as if you were made skipper of the *Titanic* just before it hit the iceberg.

If I'm Not Going to Buy a Business That's up for Sale, What Do I Do?

Every single business is really up for sale—it's just that the current owner may not know it. Everyone has a price. Telling a business owner you want to take care of him for the rest of his life is an attractive proposal—especially for someone who has perspired and struggled for years to make a business work and who probably has little or nothing in the bank for his retirement. Presenting the purchase of his business as a lifelong income can make even the most contented business owner sit up and take notice of you.

Try to decide what type of business fits your needs and abilities. Ask yourself if it's a business you'd enjoy working in. Does it fit your lifestyle? Can your family members help out? Perhaps most important, can you apply any of your previous experience to this new industry? The more you can draw on your own experience, the greater your chances of success.

Once you've come up with some ideas, start fishing for candidates. Talk to your professionals. Ask them if they know any businesses that might be available for the right price. Contact trade associations and explain what you're looking for. Call the Chamber of Commerce. Speak to friends and relatives and co-workers. Drive around and check out what stores are in your area—or in an area you'd like to relocate to.

How Do I Analyze Businesses I've Identified as Candidates?

Begin by studying the location. Only when you're convinced a location is viable should you proceed.

• Are new shopping centers opening nearby?
• What's the character of the area?
• Is there evidence of new construction?
• Is there sufficient parking?
• Are traffic routes and patterns favorable?
• What's the attitude of local government toward business?

Once you've decided the location is viable, present your case for taking care of the current owner for life. If you're unable to get him interested, don't waste your time. Move on to another candidate. But if you do get a bite, start digging for some basic information.

First, find out how long the business has existed, who founded it, and how many owners there have been. The longer a business has been around and the longer it has been in the same location, the more goodwill it should have. If ownership has turned over more than once, there could be something wrong. If the business is owned by the heirs or replacements of a founder, it will be easier to pry loose than if it's still owned by a founder who's apt to be more emotionally tied to it.

Next, try to determine if the business is profitable and if profits are increasing or decreasing. Have your accountant take a look at financial records for at least the past five years. Ask for balance sheets, income statements, and tax returns—both federal and local. Work up the ratios of the business and compare them with industry averages. Ask your accountant what you as the new owner could do to improve these ratios. Have your attorney conduct a lien and judgment search on the owners and the hard assets of the business. Check with Dun & Bradstreet and credit bureaus for additional financial background information.

Then, do some further digging:

- What's the condition of the inventory? Is the equipment in good condition?
- Contact an independent business appraiser to get a third-party view on the business's intangible value.
- Check the reputation of the business in both the industry and the community.
- Examine the terms and conditions of the lease. You can't buy goodwill if you're forced to relocate.
- Are the suppliers sound? Do they offer good service?
- How many competitors are there now and are there likely to be in the future?
- Are the employees competent, and are key people willing to remain after ownership shifts?

What Do I Do If They Say There's a "Second Set" of Books?

It's true that some small businesses try to obscure profits to avoid paying heavy taxes, making tax returns an unreliable gauge of their profits. But you can't rely on figures from a "second set" of books. Instead you and your accountant should ask for records of bank deposits. You should check the bills paid to suppliers and reconcile them with sales records. Remember, it's also possible that profits are overstated. Perhaps the owner didn't write off bad debts. Maybe his inventory is overstated or his equipment under-depreciated. Make sure to remove all the personal expenses of the previous owner—salary, perquisites, travel, and entertainment—from the financial statements and then factor in your own personal expenses.

Once I Find a Candidate Business That Looks Good, How Do I Go about Buying It?

There are two ways to buy a business: you can purchase either its balance sheet or its assets.

Purchasing a balance sheet means taking over the liabilities as well as the assets, so it's preferred by sellers. I'd suggest you just purchase the assets and have the previous owner dissolve the company and take care of any liabilities.

If you buy the balance sheet, you'll be responsible for the prior tax returns of the business or lawsuits arising from actions taken in the past. If you buy the assets, you can't be held liable for anything that happened in the past.

How Do You Determine What a Business Is Worth?

There are four ways to determine the value of a business: liquidation value, book value, market value, and formula value.

Liquidation value is the amount the tangible assets of the business would bring at auction. It's the lowest value you can assign to a business and the most desirable way to buy.

Book value is simply the value listed in the books of the business. This is an easy way to make a rough estimate on what it would cost you to buy the business.

Market value is based on rules of thumb, formulas, and principles acquired through years of experience by business appraisers and accountants. Your accountant can come up with this number for you.

Sellers will object to these three methods of determining value because they don't account for what's called "goodwill." The best way to think of goodwill is as the payment you make to the original entrepreneur for all the mistakes and problems he had while growing the business to its present level.

Unfortunately it's very difficult to quantify how much this is worth to you.

I think the best way to set a price on a business that includes fair valuation of goodwill is to determine the business's formula value. This is a fairly complex process. You'll probably have your accountant help you, but it's important you understand how it works, so I'll explain it slowly, using round numbers as examples.

(Don't feel bad if it takes reading these paragraphs a few times for you to understand the concept. Valuing businesses is a very subjective, arcane art rather than a science and has been the subject of massive studies and voluminous works. What counts is that your accountant knows what he's doing.)

First, establish the adjusted value of the business's tangible assets by subtracting the total liabilities from the total assets. But rather than using the numbers from the seller's balance sheet, make judgments based on the research you've done. Let's say you determine this is $100,000.

Next, estimate how much you could earn annually by placing that amount in some other type of investment. Let's say you figure out that you could earn $10,000 by investing that same $100,000 in a Treasury bill.

Now, add that potential earnings to the current salary you're making. If you aren't currently drawing a salary, use the salary you plan to draw as owner of the business. Let's say you're currently earning $50,000. Add that to the potential earnings of $10,000 and you come up with $60,000.

Determine the average annual net earnings of the business for the past three to five years. Net earnings is the net profit the business made before the owner took out a salary. Let's say that in 1993 the business had an annual net earnings of $69,000. In 1994 the figure was $71,000. And in 1995 it dropped down to $70,000. The average of these three numbers is $70,000.

Subtract the total of earnings power and current salary (in our example, $60,000) from the average annual net earnings of the business ($70,000 in our example). The resulting number ($10,000) is called the extra earnings power of the business.

You can use this extra earnings power figure to determine the value of the business's goodwill.

You do this by multiplying the earnings power number by a "certainty" figure. This certainty figure comes from estimating

- how unique and powerful the goodwill seems to be.
- how long it would take to bring a new business up to this performance.
- how well established the business is.

The surer it is that the business will continue in the manner it has, the higher a certainty figure you should choose. Work with a range from 1 to 5. A business that's been around for 20 years, is well-known, and has been consistently profitable gets a certainty figure of 5. A business started a year ago, with no track record of profitability, gets a certainty figure of 1.

Let's say the business you're valuing has been around for 10 years, is fairly well known, has achieved a moderate amount of goodwill, and has had steady profits for more than five years. A certainty figure of 3 would seem justified.

Multiplying the extra earnings power ($10,000) by the certainty figure (3), you'll come up with an estimate of the value of business's goodwill ($30,000).

The final step in determining formula value is to go back to the business's adjusted tangible net worth ($100,000) and add it to the value you've assigned to the business's goodwill ($30,000). The total ($130,000) is the formula value of the business.

How Much Room Is There for Negotiating the Terms of the Deal?

This is probably the single most negotiable transaction around. And it should be, considering all the assumptions and estimates and guesses you have to make.

That's why you should never pay all cash for an existing business. The seller has to in some way guarantee the claims he's made that you've been unable to substantiate. The only way he can do that is by taking back paper—in effect, giving you a mortgage on the business.

The terms of the deal may actually be more important than the actual purchase price. Obviously the longer the term and the lower the interest, the better off you are. The financial arrangements you make with the seller are limited only by law and the creativity of you, your attorney, and your accountant.

One definite part of the package, however, has to be the former owner's agreement to serve as your teacher and in-house consultant for as long as is necessary. Obviously you'll have to pay for this service, in one way or another. But how you pay is entirely up to you and the former owner.

Buying a Franchise

A franchise is a mutually beneficial financial partnership between a large organization (the franchisor) and an independent entrepreneur (the franchisee), in which the former sells the latter the right to conduct business using its name, trademarks, products, procedures, marketing plans, and/or advertising. Put more simply, a franchise is the safest way to go into business for yourself.

What Are the Advantages of Franchising?

A franchise owner has a four times greater chance to succeed than someone who starts a business from scratch and a two times greater chance to succeed than someone who buys an existing business. One recent study found that around 97% of franchises opened in the past five years are still in operation, and 85% of them are still run by the original owner.

The success of franchising as an industry continues to astound business experts. There are more than 550,000 franchise businesses in the United States, and the number increases each year. One-third of all retail sales come from franchise businesses. By 2000 that share is projected to climb to one-half.

The numbers are pretty remarkable. According to the U.S. Department of Commerce, in 1970 there were 396,000 franchised businesses in the United States, and they were responsible for sales of around $120 billion. In 1980 the number of franchised businesses grew to 442,000, and they were responsible for $326 billion in sales. And by 1990 the number of franchised businesses had grown to 533,000 establishments responsible for $716 billion in sales.

Even during recent periods of economic uncertainty, franchising has grown. In the recent recession, when most corporations and businesses were laying off people in an effort to remain afloat, franchises were enjoying a growth in revenues of around 7%. Just in 1992 the franchising industry spawned more than 20,000 new businesses and 100,000 new jobs. According to figures from the International Franchise Association, by 1992 there were 558,000 franchised businesses in the United States, generating $803 billion in sales.

But it's more than the numbers that makes franchising such a good bet today. By luck or design, franchising capitalizes on a number of trends sweeping American society.

- The increasing mobility of our society means we're valuing familiarity more than ever. When you're new to a town it's comforting to be able to turn to someone or something you're experienced with: a Decorating Den, for example, or a McDonald's.
- As America becomes more and more culturally diverse, it opens up additional opportunities for franchises, which are especially adept at identifying and targeting niche markets.
- Similarly, as we become more of a service economy, niches will develop for new businesses to provide new services . . . and once again franchises will probably lead the way.
- The power of advertising and marketing will grow in the infor-

mation age, and franchise businesses have the advantage of having a national advertising campaign to support their local efforts.

- The increasing globalization of our economy means it will help to have links, in one form or another, to businesses in other nations. Franchise businesses have been the leaders in expanding into new global markets.

What Are the Disadvantages of Franchising?

Franchising definitely has a downside, too.

- You're going to have to work extremely hard—harder, probably, than you work at your current job.
- You're going to be under just as much, if not more, stress as you are today.
- While you may get a good income from this business, you won't be able to pass it along to your kids, since, as you'll soon see, most franchisors retain the right to buy the business back from you or your heirs.
- You're not going to have complete control over what you do— if the franchisor demands you wear a funny little hat when you're working, you've got to go along with him.
- Finally, the surge in franchising has spawned not only thousands of successful franchisors, but also thousands of con artists looking to steal you blind.

What Type of Franchise Should I Investigate?

There are four types of franchises:

- Manufacturer-retailer franchises in which a manufacturer sells a retailer the right to stock and sell its products. The best examples are automobile dealerships.
- Manufacturer-wholesaler franchises in which a manufacturer sells a wholesaler either a finished product or the ingredients to

finish a product, and then the wholesaler distributes it. The best examples are soft-drink distributorships.

- Wholesaler-retailer franchises in which the wholesaler sells the retailer the right to carry the products it distributes. The best examples are Radio Shack stores.
- Business format franchises in which the franchisor sells a trade name, identity, and a method of doing business to a franchisee. These are the most common franchises (and fastest growing) and include chains ranging from McDonald's to Holiday Inn.

It's this final type that you should concentrate on. By purchasing a good business format franchise, you'll be buying a system that's been proven successful. An experienced business format franchisor will be able to pass along his own knowledge, compensating for your lack of experience. By buying a business format franchise, you'll be able to take advantage of a large organization's marketing and research and development efforts. Since most business format franchises target market niches, you'll be well positioned to weather any economic downturns. Finally, there are business format franchises that are very affordable, some can be run from home offices or automobiles, and others can be operated part-time.

What Industries Should I Look to Buy a Franchise In?

The two biggest industries in business format franchising are restaurants and convenience stores. Both have their advantages and disadvantages.

Restaurant franchising is growing exponentially. It's not just the province of fast-food places anymore—today there are sit-down family-style restaurant franchises as well. The demand for affordable restaurant meals seems able to weather economic downturns. With the population of the United States constantly shifting from one region to another there are always new opportunities for restaurant franchises.

There are several problems with restaurant franchises, however: they're comparatively expensive (an Arby's, for instance, requires a total investment of from $550,000 to $850,000); the competition is fierce; you may have to relocate to an area that doesn't currently have the franchise you're considering; and experience is definitely a plus in restaurant operations (that's why McDonald's sends its franchisees to its own college for training).

Convenience store franchises are also growing dramatically, probably because they serve a clearly defined market niche. Most are quite flexible, allowing them to adjust to changing consumer tastes and demands. The better organizations provide extensive training, pretty much compensating for lack of experience. Convenience stores generally require very small staffs, so you won't have a large payroll.

However, there are some definite downsides to convenience store franchises. What's convenient for your customers may not be convenient for you. Seven-day weeks and 24-hour days don't sound like my idea of fun. And don't count on relying on others too much—convenience stores really need hands-on management. Finally, many supermarkets are trying to fight the trend toward convenience stores, so there may be more competition in the future.

I suppose what I'm suggesting is that rather than picking an industry because it's hot, you should select one that fits your own needs and abilities. Just as you didn't pick a business to buy just because it was up for sale, neither should you pick a franchise because it's all the rage. Instead ask yourself if it's a business you'd enjoy working in. Does it fit your lifestyle? Can you afford to buy a franchise in the industry without courting disaster? Can your family members help out in the business? And can you apply any of your previous experience to this new industry? I know I'm beginning to sound like a broken record, but I'll repeat it once again: The more you can draw on your own experience, the greater your chances of success.

(For more information on selecting industries, take a look at Chapter 6.)

How Can I Judge Candidate Franchises?

The key to narrowing your choices is to conduct some extensive research. While much of the information will be provided by the disclosure documents the franchisor will provide, some can come only from independent research. Don't cut corners in your investigating. This is probably the largest or second largest purchase you'll ever make, and much of your future depends on it being a savvy buy.

Begin by investigating each franchisor individually.

- Do you like and trust him?
- Do you agree with his business philosophy?
- Is he in good financial shape?
- Is he involved in any current litigation?
- How long has he been in business?
- Has he ever sold franchises in a different industry?
- Has he ever declared bankruptcy?
- Do you have confidence in his plans for the future?
- Is he more concerned with selling new franchises or supporting those he's already sold?
- What's his reputation in the industry?
- Is he a member of an industry association?
- Do you think he's open to your input and ideas?

Then, try to evaluate the product or service the franchise offers.

- Is its trademark or name recognizable?
- Do you think it's marketable in your area?
- Is it a fad, or does it have the potential to be marketable for the long term?

Next, do some digging into how well the franchise system operates.

- How many hours do franchisees put in?
- Are the franchisees members of an association?
- Is there a franchisee advisory committee?
- Is start-up training provided?
- Is ongoing training provided?
- Do you have to purchase your supplies from the franchisor?
- Do you have any choice in the products or services you sell?
- How can you get out of the business?
- How can you renew your franchise agreement?
- Are you allowed to expand?
- How many franchisees have left or sold their units?
- Why have they left?

Try to speak with other franchisees. A reputable franchisor will provide you with names and telephone numbers of contacts.

- How's their relationship with the franchisor?
- Have they had any problems?
- Do they think the franchisor cares about their success?
- Has the franchisor been a help or a hindrance?

Finally, explore the financial elements of each candidate.

- How much is the franchise fee?
- What are the start-up costs?
- What are the working capital requirements?
- How much are the royalty fees?

How Do I Figure out How Much Money I Can Make?

While few (less than 15%) franchisors provide explicit information on how much money you can make, it's not too difficult to use the numbers they *do* provide to come up with your own estimate.

Somewhere in the financial disclosure documents you'll receive there's a figure for how much income the franchisor is receiving in royalties. Divide that number by the percentage he charges as a royalty rate. This will give you the total gross sales of all his franchisees. Divide that figure by the total number of franchise units and you'll have an approximation of the gross sales per unit. Finally, take the stated estimates of operational costs and subtract them from the gross sales per unit figure. The result is a ball park figure for what your gross profit will be.

How Can I Tell If a Franchisor Is Honest?

Obviously there's no single surefire sign of a crooked franchisor. However, there are some things you can take as warning signals:

- Being asked to pay for the offering circular
- Incomplete or inaccurate information in the circular
- Hesitation about answering questions regarding information that's missing from the circular
- Claims of being prohibited by law from disclosing information
- Failing to provide the names of those who have left the company recently
- Failing to provide a copy of the franchise agreement with the circular
- Lack of audited financial statements for the three previous years
- Pressure to sign or to pay any fees before or shortly after receiving information
- Promises inconsistent with information in the circular

Can I Negotiate the Terms of the Franchise Agreement?

Franchise agreements, like all contracts, are entirely negotiable. However, the extent to which franchisees are able to make changes to franchise agreements varies from franchisor to franchisor. Some franchisors whose units are in big demand may refuse to make any changes. Other franchisors, who are hungry to expand, may be very flexible. The one thing for certain is that you should hire an attorney experienced in franchising to represent your interests.

Before you sign any agreement with a franchisor, you and your attorney should make sure

- you understand and agree with all the terms and clauses.
- the trademark and trade names are registered and can be used where you intend to do business.
- your business is clearly distinguished from the franchisor's business.
- the agreement clearly states what you're getting in exchange for your franchise fee.
- you're satisfied with the start-up and ongoing training outlined in the agreement.
- you're given sufficient time to get the business launched.
- advertising terms are described fully.
- you're satisfied with the terms for selling your unit or terminating the agreement.

What Is the Best Way to Finance the Purchase of a Franchise?

There are lots of places you can turn for the money to buy a franchise. Obviously you can use your own funds or borrow money from family or friends. You can take out a personal loan or a home-equity loan. But the best bet, as far as I'm concerned, is to turn to the franchisor for help. About one-third of franchisors provide some form of direct or third-party financing for their franchisees.

There are some definite advantages to getting your money from the franchisor. He's already pretty confident in you (otherwise he wouldn't be selling you a franchise), so it shouldn't be too difficult to get the money. Getting the funds directly from him will also speed up the whole process. Finally, being your source of funds as well as your franchisor increases his stake in your success.

The only real disadvantage is that by borrowing from your

franchisor, you're giving him more power over you. However, I think that's outweighed by all the advantages.

Relocating to Start a Business

One possible advantage to both buying an existing business and buying a franchise is that you can relocate to another area. Joel Garreau, author of *Edge City: Life on the New Frontier* (Doubleday), suggests that if you're looking for a new area to move to in order to go into business, you should look for places

- where the local police and teachers can afford to live in the community.
- that have air connections to major cities.
- where it's possible to schedule a breakfast meeting without fear of being late.

You can use statistics to make a more specific investigation into areas. *American Demographics* has studied the numbers and come up with the best markets for various industries. You can do the same by using census data. Here's a sampling from the *American Demographics* study (you can find the complete report in the January 1996 issue):

- Affluent metropolitan areas spend the most on eating out and would therefore be the best places to open restaurants. The 15 metro areas that devote the largest share of household spending on food away from home are, in descending order, San Jose, CA; Middlesex-Somerset-Hunterdon, NJ; Anchorage, AK; Nassau-Suffolk, NY; Orange County, CA; Washington D.C.-MD-VA-WV; Ventura, CA; Honolulu, HI; Dutchess County, NY; Bergen-Passaic, NJ; New Haven-Bridgeport-Stamford-

Danbury-Waterbury, CT; Oakland, CA; Newark, NJ; Hartford, CT; and Trenton, NJ. The five worst places to open a restaurant would be Cumberland, MD-WV; Ocala, FL; Johnston, PA; Brownsville-Harlingen-San Benito, TX; and McAllen-Edinburg-Mission, TX.

- If you're thinking of opening a smoke shop, look to younger southern towns that have the highest density of likely smokers. The 15 metro areas that have the highest average spending on tobacco are, in descending order, El Paso, TX; New Orleans, LA; San Antonio, TX; McAllen-Edinburg-Mission, TX; Memphis, TN-AR-MS; Las Vegas, NV-AZ; Nashville, TN; Greensboro-Winston-Salem-High Point, NC; Norfolk-Virginia Beach-Newport News, VA-NC; Brownsville-Harlingen-San Benito, TX; Miami, FL; Houston, TX; Salt Lake City-Ogden, UT; Columbus, OH; and Portland-Vancouver, OR-WA. The five worst places to open a smoke shop would be Trenton, NJ; Rochester, MN; Punta Gorda, FL; Barnstable-Yarmouth, MA; and Naples, FL.

- If you're thinking of opening a health care-related business, you'll do best looking for an area with a high concentration of older Americans, regardless of income. The 15 metro areas that have the highest average spending on health care are, in descending order, Sarasota-Bradenton, FL; Punta Gorda, FL; Tampa-St. Petersburg-Clearwater, FL; West Palm Beach-Boca Raton, FL; Monmouth-Ocean, NJ; Fort Lauderdale, FL; Pittsburgh, PA; Fort Myers-Cape Coral, FL; Bergen-Passaic, NJ; Nassau-Suffolk, NY; Fort Pierce-Port St. Lucie, FL; Scranton-Wilkes Barre-Hazelton, PA; Chicago, IL; Ocala, FL; and Los Angeles-Long Beach, CA. The five areas where a health care business is most likely to go belly up are Gainesville, FL; Iowa City, IA; Lawrence, KS; Jacksonville, NC; and Bryan-College Station, TX.

Selecting an Industry

Finally, it doesn't hurt to pay attention to the numbers when you're looking to start a business in a different industry. Economist Bruce Phillips of the Small Business Administration has studied the failure rates in small business-dominated industries. He has come up with a list of the five most dangerous industries to enter and the five safest.

THE FIVE MOST DANGEROUS

- Amusement and recreational services (far and away the highest failure rate)
- Oil and gas extraction companies
- Lumber and manufacturing firms
- General building contractors
- Furniture and home furnishing stores

THE FIVE LEAST DANGEROUS

- Personal service companies
- Insurance agencies and brokerages
- Legal service companies
- Health service companies
- Educational service companies (far and away the lowest failure rate)

The Story of Alex McCloskey

I met Alex McCloskey back when I opened my first law office on Long Island, New York. He was a young aerospace draftsman who came to me for help in buying his first home—a typical Levittown starter house. Over the years, despite my moving into New York City and Alex's moving farther out east on Long Island, we stayed in touch. I worked with him and his wife, Maria, on the sale of their Levittown house and the purchase of a bigger place in Coram. I helped him draft a will and review his financial plans when his children were born. That's why I wasn't surprised when, after about 10 years, I got a message that Alex called my office. What surprised me was the reason for his call.

After putting in more than 35 years as an aerospace draftsman, Alex wanted to start over. He was tired of his work and tired of Long Island . . . but he wasn't tired of working. On the telephone he confessed to me that he had always harbored the dream of running a little sandwich shop. Now he and Maria, who had worked for 30 years in the cafeteria of a high school, wanted my advice about moving down to Florida and starting their own deli/luncheonette. Since I was going to be out on the island the next week visiting another client, I arranged to meet Alex and Maria for breakfast at a diner we all used to frequent.

When I met them I was surprised at how little they had changed. Sure, Maria was a bit grayer and Alex was wider around the middle, but they both appeared to be as lively as they ever were. It was clear that neither of them relished the idea of being inactive. They might not have loved their work, but they loved working. Without dampening their enthusiasm too much, I explained that starting from scratch on their own in an entirely new business was a real gamble, one that might not make sense at their ages. I arranged for them to come to my office for a formal meeting.

At that meeting the three of us went over their needs and

wants, their finances, and their options. Both wanted to work, full-time. They didn't see any way else to live. Still, they didn't want to answer to anyone else. After taking orders most of their lives, they'd had it with bosses. But at the same time, neither had much confidence in their own creativity. However, they definitely wanted to work together. They had spent most of their younger days apart and wanted to spend the rest of them together.

They had saved up some money over the years—around $30,000—but were counting primarily on their combined pensions, which would be providing them with a very nice retirement income of about $30,000. Their mortgage was fully paid up, and after buying a place in Florida, they'd probably have about a $45,000 profit on the sale of their house in Coram.

After looking at the possibilities, they decided to investigate franchise opportunities. The analytical process of investigating franchises appealed to the draftsman in Alex. And the greater security they offered appealed to Maria's conservatism. With their spirits high, I put them in touch with another attorney who specializes in franchising.

Eight months later a huge package from Florida arrived at my office. When I unwrapped it I saw it was a cooler. Inside the cooler, packed in dry ice, were a dozen submarine sandwiches. Alex and Maria had just opened a franchised sandwich shop in an up-and-coming town on the east coast of Florida.

Two months later I was able to stop off at Alex's shop while I was down in Florida visiting my parents. Both he and Maria were ecstatic. They're working hard but loving the interaction with people. They're both working in the shop and have hired some other semiretirees as their staff. Alex is happier assembling subs than he ever was drawing aircraft engines, and Maria still gets the same joy dishing up food as she did at the school cafeteria—except now the clientele is a bit older.

For More Information

For sources of more information on buying an existing business and franchising, see Appendix Two on page 203.

CHAPTER 11

Go Back to School and Get a Part-Time Job

THE FACTS AT A GLANCE

- Feasibility: 2
- Risk: 2
- Problems it *will* solve: too much stress, not enough time, not rewarding emotionally, maxed out in company, maxed out in industry, no longer challenging, unhealthy environment
- Time: depends on willingness to sacrifice, ability to borrow, amount of savings, and size of spousal income

Going back to school is probably the dream option. It's the ultimate way to start over because you're literally starting from square one. If you couple it with getting a part-time job in the field you're being educated for, it will solve every problem except for lack of financial reward. It doesn't have much inherent risk. There aren't very many external roadblocks, so it's quite feasible. So why do so few people pursue it? Because it requires clearing a hurdle that, while not insurmountable, is darn close to it. That hurdle, of course, is money or, more specifically, stream of income.

How Do You Replace the Income You're Giving Up?

You can borrow money for college tuition through any one of a dozen different programs. But where do you come up with the money to keep food on your table, keep clothes on your child's back, and keep your medical insurance coverage? There are really only three sources.

FIRST, YOU CAN TAP INTO YOUR OWN SAVINGS

If you've money set aside for your retirement, or your child's college education, you can shift it to your own reeducation. This presupposes that you've got enough money to draw on and that you're willing to sacrifice your kid's education for your own.

SECOND, YOU CAN RELY ON A SPOUSE'S INCOME

By going on an austerity budget and streamlining your lifestyle, you may be able to get by on your spouse's income and a part-time job of your own. Of course, this presupposes you've got a spouse, he or she is willing to support your efforts, and you can both live on one income.

THIRD, YOU CAN BORROW THE MONEY TO LIVE ON FROM FAMILY AND FRIENDS

The idea is to approach them the same way you would to borrow money to start your own business (see Chapter 9) but instead use the money to keep your head afloat while in school. The arrangement would require some type of interest and payment plan, theoretically coming out of the increased earnings you'll have with your new education.

Pursue Vocational, Not Avocational, Learning

That's really the key to making this option work: increased earnings. In order to justify the kinds of sacrifices you're requiring of yourself and others to make this option work, you need to know that you'll come out of this educational venture with greater earnings potential than when you went in. That means you'll either be trained for a more secure field, prepared to enter a growing industry, or schooled in a more lucrative profession.

Unless you're independently wealthy, there's no way I think you can justify going back to school simply for the joys of learning. Yes, learning is a wonderful thing, with intrinsic value of its own. It's something we all should pursue throughout our lives. But such an approach to learning cannot take the place of a job or career.

If you love art history, by all means take courses in it at night or when you retire. However, I can't agree with you giving up your job to get a master's in it. In effect, this option should really be an interim step before either pursuing a job in a new career or industry or starting a business.

173

Selecting a School

If you've got the kind of financial cushion you need and you're ready to pursue an educational course that will eventually improve your work life, your next big decision is to select a school or program. Once again there are scores of books on this topic, so I'll start by suggesting you look at the works listed at the back of this book. Beyond that, however, you should focus on six factors.

Look for a college that enables you to minimize your family's expenses and maximize your family's income. That means a school nearby so your spouse can keep his or her job and, if possible, one accessible by mass transportation so you don't have to spend a fortune commuting by car.

Look for a college that will give you the maximum credit for your life and work experience. The more credit they offer in exchange for your experiences, the less you'll pay in tuition and the quicker you'll be back in the job market earning money to pay back your loans.

Look for a college that has special programs for older students. Returning students like you are in demand. Colleges love you, not only for your wallet, but for what you bring to the classroom: maturity, wisdom, and diversity. The college you choose should have some special programs to help you make the transition to the academic world.

Look for a college that offers extensive work-study programs and/or internships. In order to maximize your time and perhaps ease the financial burden on your spouse, you'll be working while going to school, preferably in the field you'd like to enter. Make sure the school you select has work-study and internship programs that will help you.

Look for a college that has an excellent job placement office. Since you're older you're going to be facing an uphill battle getting a job in your new field. Make sure the school you choose has a good placement office that has experience placing older students. Even if you're going to be starting your own business, a good placement office will be helpful in building up a network for you.

Look for a college that offers the flexibility and adaptability you need. Returning students like you require a great deal more flexibility from colleges than traditional students do. Most first-year MBA students don't have to worry about missing an exam to attend their daughter's high school graduation. You need a college that is flexible enough to recognize your special needs and bend to them, rather than forcing you to fit into its rigid set of rules and regulations.

Finally, if you're really able to pull off this option, you should count your blessings—you're one of only a handful of people. I envy you.

The Story of Wendy Mitchell

Wendy Mitchell always had two great loves (three if you count her husband, Bob): children and library research. She went to college to study education and spent the first six years of her post-college life as an elementary school teacher. Then, after she and her husband had their first child, she realized her feelings about teaching, not children, had changed. That's when she came to me.

Wendy told me that before she had her daughter, Charlotte, teaching satisfied a real need in her. But once she'd had a little girl of her own to teach and nurture and love, she began to feel there were other needs she had that weren't being fulfilled. She wanted to do something that involved research, something that was more satisfying intellectually.

She and Bob and I spent a long time going over the possibilities. We calculated that if they cut back on their lifestyle and got lots of baby-sitting help from their two mothers, they could get by on Bob's salary alone. He was a salesman for a major shoe manufacturer and earned around $55,000 including commissions. Their mortgage payment was pretty hefty, around $1,100 a month. But thanks to Bob's company car and a solid benefits package, their other costs weren't too exorbitant. That meant they could afford for Wendy to go back to school.

They knew, however, that they needed Wendy to go back to work fairly quickly if they were going to save enough money to send their daughter to college, too. Wendy and Bob had no savings to speak of—just his 401(k) and about $1,500 in a savings account they were going to use for a vacation. They also wanted something that either paid well enough for them to be able to afford child care or was flexible enough for Wendy to work out some creative schedule. They knew that while Wendy's mom would love sitting with Charlotte every day, she wasn't up to it physically. And Bob's mom, who was happy to watch Charlotte every other day, was planning on moving south in a year or two.

We had trouble coming up with a solution until one day when I was running behind schedule. Wendy was waiting outside my office, talking to my paralegal, Shannon, when she realized the answer was literally right before our eyes all along.

Wendy went back to school full-time to become a paralegal. While it was tough for awhile, she and Bob were able to get through the trauma of having only one income, thanks in no small part to their mothers. Now Wendy's a trained paralegal, earning more than she did as a teacher, working on a flexible schedule that lets her work at home and take care of Charlotte on Mondays and Fridays. Her mom watches Charlotte Tuesdays, Wednesdays, and Thursdays when Wendy's at the office. Wendy's waking up each morning eager to go to work. And she and Bob are starting to put some money away for their future.

For More Information

For more sources of information on selecting and paying for a college education, see Appendix Three on page 227.

CHAPTER 12

Downshift

The Facts at a Glance
- Feasibility: 1
- Risk: 1
- Problems it *will* solve: too much stress, not enough time, not rewarding emotionally, unhealthy environment
- Time: 12 months to tie up loose ends

Downshifting is the starting over option that has gotten the most media attention in the past couple of years. As defined by the media, downshifting involves radically shifting the emphasis in your life away from your work to your personal life and, in the process, renouncing a great many material comforts.

Downshifting is being promoted as a more spiritually enlightened approach to life. Rather than worrying about advancing in their careers or buying a new stereo, these downshifters are concerned with saving Mother Earth, raising their children, or healing their communities. It all sounds so wonderful, doesn't it?

Obviously lots of Americans think so. According to a survey cited in a recent issue of *Utne Reader*, 64% of Americans fantasize about quitting their jobs to live on a desert island or travel the world. I agree that this is a great fantasy. I've had it, too. But while I hate to be the one to wake you from this dream, downshifting doesn't always make financial sense.

Radical Downshifting Has Many Problems

First, it doesn't take into account the demands placed on you by your responsibilities to children and parents who may need and want those material benefits you're giving up. In effect, you're forcing your dependents to downsize, too, whether they want to or not. Sure, maybe it's more valuable to provide spiritual values than a new Sega video system to your kids. But let's say your daughter is 16 and has been planning on going to the Yale School of Drama her whole life. How fair is it for you to now turn around and tell her she'll be better off feeding chickens in Idaho or raising the whole tuition bill herself?

Second, it's justifiable only if you actually replace the role work played in your life with some other primary focus. A life without purpose is just as wasted as a life that's unexamined. It's clearly wonderful to give up being an accountant and volunteer for VISTA or the Peace Corps. It's also great if you can give up your career as a magazine editor to dedicate yourself to raising your son or daughter. But is it so terrific and noble to give up your job to just walk along the beach or study the sunset?

I hate to be cynical about the downshifting movement, but it seems to me that lots of the people who have actually down-shifted radically have replaced their old careers with a new career: encouraging others to downshift. Through books, newsletters, or groups, some (not all) are making more money now that they've downshifted than they ever did before.

Third, most of the people who are doing this radical down-shifting had previously led extremely successful, materially filled lives. Sure, in the end it may not have been spiritually satisfying for them to have a BMW, travel to Europe every year, have a summer home on Martha's Vineyard, and work in a corner office. But they certainly got to enjoy those things for a while, didn't they?

It's a lot easier to say spending every April in Paris isn't all it's cracked up to be after you've done it for five years in a row. When your vacation is a long weekend at your parents' house in North Carolina, and your car needs a new transmission, and your house needs a new roof, it's a lot harder to scoff at materialism.

I guess what I'm saying is that it appears that in order to give up luxury you've first got to have it . . . and have it long enough to find it boring. That's a problem most of us, including me, would like to have.

Fourth, I can't help but feel that part of this whole movement is copping out. Deep down I think that a lot of the people who currently find downshifting so attractive are actually rationaliz-ing the fact that they're unemployed or underemployed. It's a classic trait of the baby boom generation to take whatever cir-cumstance presents itself at any one time and say it's the most valid. This downshifting movement is, I'm afraid, just a way to make it chic to be a laid-off, former yuppie.

Having said all that, and having probably alienated a lot of you in the process, I do have some good things to say about down-shifting. I think it can be a rational choice and a pragmatic option, if it's done for the right reasons and in a less radical manner.

Downshifting is one of only two options that definitely will solve the problems of excessive stress and not having enough time (the other is going back to school—see Chapter 11). So if those are truly your primary problems, you don't really have many options to pursue.

Downshifting Can Solve the Problem of Excessive Stress

There are, of course, other less radical ways of combating this stress. Some of these ways are healthy—exercise, hobbies—and some aren't—drinking, smoking, drug abuse. If you've already tried other healthy ways of combating stress and still find yourself facing the existential black pit, then maybe you *do* need to shift to a less stressful existence. And if you're turning to unhealthy ways of dealing with stress, certainly some radical change is in order. Just be sure you've tried power walking or ceramics before you give up your job, sell your possessions, and buy a Winnebago.

In addition, make sure the stress isn't an innate part of your personality. I know people who don't feel stressed out even though they're in highly stressful occupations. And I know others who, if they did drop out and buy a Winnebago, would get stressed out over whether it would fit under every overpass on the route they were about to drive. In other words, if you are by your very nature a stressed-out person, it's therapy you need, not downshifting.

Downshifting Can Solve the Problem of Not Enough Time

The pursuit of more time is pretty easy to justify.

- In a July 1994 Gallup poll, one-third of those surveyed said they'd take a 20% cut in pay if they could work fewer hours.
- Juliet B. Schor, author of *The Overworked American,* found that

an employed person in 1987 put in 163 more extra hours on the job than an employed person in 1969.

• The value of time is just about to reach parity with the value of money in real-life terms, according to studies by John Robinson, a sociologist at the University of Maryland.

My only caveat here is that you intend to use that time for something more than, or just as important as, generating an income. That judgment is a personal one. However, it's clear to most everyone that raising a child is just as important as advancing in your career—perhaps more so. If you're pursuing more time so you can paint watercolor landscapes, then you're talking about retiring, not downshifting. Unless, of course, you can make a decent living selling those watercolors.

Even if your reasons for downshifting are justifiable, I think it's more practical if you pursue less radical versions of it. Let me offer some suggestions.

Move to an Area with a Lower Cost of Living and a Better Quality of Life

Relocation expert James Angelini notes that a couple with one child, earning $70,000 a year in San Francisco, California, can cut their cost of living almost in half by moving to Austin, Texas, or Atlanta, Georgia. (For $190 his company, Right Choice, Inc., 800-872-2294, will analyze the financial impact of moving from one city to another.)

Of course, to relocate you'll either have to get another job, start your own business, deal with what's apt to be a longer commute (hence less time and maybe more stress), or negotiate some kind of telecommuting arrangement.

If any of those sound both acceptable and possible, and you're looking for quality of life as well as a lower cost of living, consider this list of things to look for, developed by Joel Garreau, author of *Edge City: Life on the New Frontier* (Doubleday):

- No reliance on government tenants
- Antigrowth or antidevelopment movements
- Investments in museums, streetscapes, mass transit, and public parks
- Strong public/private partnerships
- Commercial construction taking place
- Imaginative retrofitting, such as turning an old school building into a shopping mall/office/apartment complex
- Wealthy minorities
- Programs that make life easier for parents
- Ethnic restaurants and independent bookstores
- Places where people pick up their morning coffee at a local coffee shop or bakery rather than a McDonald's drive-through

Give Up One of Your Two Incomes If You're a Two-Income Couple

Many of the advocates of downshifting indicate that the second paycheck in many two-income families goes almost entirely to child care, taxes, commuting, take-out dinners, clothing, dry cleaning, and other costs directly attributable to holding down the job. If that's the case in your two-income family, you could conceivably downshift and perhaps increase your time and decrease your stress level by having one of you stay home full-time.

Of course, it's important you give this issue some serious study and discuss the emotional as well as financial ramifications.

While giving up a second paycheck may make financial sense

today, it may not in the future. You should eventually get a salary increase. That could tip the balance in favor of work. Once your children reach a certain age child care costs level off. If your child gets a part-time job, they could even decline.

Leaving the workforce temporarily could force a permanent change in your life. As many women who left work to stay home and raise their children have learned, it's very tough to get back on the career ladder once you've gotten off. Before you give up that income, make sure you're not going to have second thoughts in 10 years.

There are less radical options, such as becoming a telecommuter, that could trim some of the costs associated with work without giving up the related income.

Last but not least, for many people work isn't just an income. It can be something that gives life meaning or allows for creativity. If that's the case, the added value from the job must be factored into every decision.

Give Up an Expensive Luxury Asset

Time is the hidden cost in many purchases. In order to afford the cost of whatever it is you're buying, you have to put in the extra hours to earn the money. When you examine the ownership of luxury assets in this way, some of them may no longer make sense. For instance, to afford the mortgage on your weekend home you may have to work all day Saturday and half on Sunday. Even if you're able to do the work up at the weekend house, is it worth the effort simply to have another workplace? If you bought a sailboat or a vacation house so the whole family could be together, and you're stuck in the office earning the money to pay for it rather than spending time with the family on the boat or at the beach house, the purchase was a mistake.

Become a Teacher Rather Than a Practitioner

I have a great deal of respect for educators, but (you knew there was a "but" coming, didn't you) teaching can offer a less stressful, less time-consuming career path.

Sure, there can be stress in teaching, especially if you're working with primary and secondary school students. And yes, it can take time to prepare lesson plans and grade papers and tests. But I believe teaching on the college level has less stress and takes less time than comparable, nonteaching positions.

Institutions of higher learning, ranging from local junior colleges to Ivy League universities, are hungry for adjunct faculty members who can teach individual courses based on their professional experiences. Generally such positions are paid per course, there's no tenure potential, and there are probably few benefits other than getting office space and use of the coffee machine and telephone.

The advantage to the university is that they don't have to pay much money to get someone who's arguably an expert. The advantage for the adjunct professor is that there's considerable psychological and emotional reward, and a surprising level of status, to go along with little stress and not much time requirement.

There are also lecturer positions available at most colleges and universities. These are tougher to get but generally offer benefits and a salary rather than a per/course fee.

The best means to work your way into these kind of opportunities is to make yourself known to the relevant department and say that you're available as a guest lecturer.

Professors love to bring in people from the "real world" to talk to their students. Not only does it give the professor a day off from lecturing (see, I told you it wasn't the toughest job in the world), but it provides a fresh perspective that can be enlightening for the students.

Serve as a guest lecturer a few times, do a good job, announce your availability for any adjunct positions, and the next time a professor goes on sabbatical you'll get a telephone call.

There are also programs in 41 states and the District of Columbia that provide alternative teacher accreditation. These usually require you to take night classes in education to complement your experience and previous degree.

However, I wouldn't consider taking such a step to be downshifting. There can be a lot of stress in teaching precollege students, as I noted earlier. There's also a lot more preparation time involved in teaching multiple classes, each with a predetermined syllabus, than in teaching one or two college lecture courses.

The Story of Eddie Lewis

I don't think you'd actually classify Eddie as a downshifter, but he's the client of mine who comes closest to illustrating this option.

Eddie and wife Debbie are both writers in their late twenties. They met while attending college in upstate New York. They were working for magazines in New York City when they came to see me about buying a home. At the time they were renting a one-bedroom apartment in Brooklyn and taking the subway to work.

They longed to buy a house somewhere outside the city in an area where there was some scenic beauty. It didn't have to be big—they weren't planning on having children. But still, that's not easy to come by in metropolitan New York. Lovely areas close to the city are very expensive—far more than Eddie and Debbie could have afforded on their combined $70,000 total income. Attractive areas where they could afford a home were so far away, they'd spend most of their time commuting rather than enjoying where they lived. So despite being excellent at what they did, they didn't make enough money to be able to afford to buy the kind of home they wanted in the kind of area they wanted.

As the three of us sat around talking, the subject of relocating came up. They both talked glowingly about the isolated small city where they had gone to college. Its major industry was higher education, so it had a surprising amount of culture and ethnic diversity. It was in a beautiful geographic area, too. What was holding them back from moving there? I asked. The answer, of course, was money.

But after only a couple of sessions I was able to help them plan out a way to solve that problem. First, we calculated how much it would cost Eddie and Debbie to live in that upstate community. Based on their leasing one good four-wheel-drive car for around $350 a month, on their paying about $1,200 each month for a mortgage, and on the other numbers they came up with through their research, we determined they would need an income of about $50,000 to live there. In addition, they'd need to have around $30,000 saved up for a down payment and their moving expenses.

While they might be able to land jobs upstate that paid them enough money to live there, it was doubtful they'd be able to continue their careers as writers, which they clearly wanted to do. My suggestion was that they start developing their own freelance writing businesses while keeping their jobs, go on an austerity budget, put away as much money as they could, and see if they could meet their goals that way. After a year of freelancing on the side, they were able to put away $14,000. Eddie felt secure that he could earn about $30,000 a year freelancing. Debbie wasn't so sure of her own ability to bring in the other $20,000 they needed. They kept at it for another year, saving an additional $12,000. Debbie's confidence climbed. Eddie was able to sell a book. The advance, coupled with their $26,000 in savings was enough to empower Debbie to make the leap of faith.

Today Eddie and Debbie both live in a place they love. They

left their jobs at the magazines and went into business for themselves, doing freelance writing. They're living richer lives on less money than they were making before. In fact, I got a call from Eddie the other day: they're thinking of buying a big old farmhouse that just came on the market. It costs less than half what a studio apartment in New York City would have cost them.

For More Information

For more sources of information on downshifting, see Appendix Four on page 229.

CHAPTER 13

Stay Where You Are

THE FACTS AT A GLANCE

- Feasibility: 1
- Risk: 1
- Problems it *will* solve: none
- Time: none

Having decided that the best thing for you to do is to stay where you are, I've two important messages for you:

- You should look on your choice as a matter of refocusing rather than settling.
- This doesn't mean you can rest on your laurels—you still have to start over.

There's No Place Like Home

Just because you've gone through the exercises in the first part of this book and discovered the best thing for you to do is stay where you are doesn't mean the exercise was wasted. Far from it. It's been as valuable as if you were heading out in an entirely different direction.

It's easy to become complacent about the familiar. Couples who have been married for years need constantly to strive to keep their relationship fresh and exciting or else they risk falling into a rut. Once in a rut you can begin to take your husband or wife for granted.

What has happened to you is the same thing that happened to Dorothy in *The Wizard of Oz*. You thought your job was terrible . . . until you took the time to examine the alternatives. After you looked around at what there was over the job rainbow, you suddenly realized there's no place like home.

This is a very common response to the self-examination and analysis I outlined in the earlier chapters. I'd say that at least half of my clients, after going through the exercises I prescribe, end up right where you are now.

Let me tell you about just one. Debbie Merton came to me depressed and unhappy. She felt as if her job as a clothing buyer were a dead end. She knew there was little or no security in the position. She hadn't gotten a salary increase in two years. And worrying about the latest women's fashions no longer was as exciting as when she'd first started out. She was bored.

But after going through the exercises outlined in the first five chapters of this book, Debbie rediscovered all the things she loved about her career and her job. She loved the travel and the exciting cycle of seasonal fashion shows. She loved the freedom the department store gave her to come and go pretty much as she pleased. Sure, she'd like to think about things other than hemlines and colors occasionally, but in the final analysis that wasn't worth the risk of changing jobs or careers. By analyzing her situation from a new perspective, Debbie was able to refocus on positive factors that had become overshadowed by a few annoyances.

This refocusing is valuable, but it's not enough. Just because you're staying put doesn't mean you shouldn't start over. If you don't free yourself from the complacency that clouded your judgment, you risk getting fired from the job you just realized you want to keep.

Starting over While Staying Put

Everyone knows that the traditional rule "last hired, first fired" has been abandoned. Today top executives meet with their number crunchers and managers and decide which of their employees are "adding value" to the organization's products, services, sales, or operations. Just "doing your job" is no longer enough. Most of the people let go in the past few years were doing their jobs fine, but that wasn't good enough.

You'd think that determining who's "adding value" would be a very logical, almost mathematical process. It's not. Sure, a handful of companies are able to measure productivity and efficiency and profitability, but even those have a hard time applying those measurements to individual employees. The decision of whether or not you're adding value to a company or business is a subjective one, based primarily on the perceptions of your immediate supervisor.

During your first few months in this job you were probably the dream employee. You had unlimited energy. You were enthusiastic. You dressed well. You smiled and had a pleasant word to say to everyone. You sought out responsibility and offered suggestions and opinions. You were the apple of your supervisor's eye.

But little by little and bit by bit, things changed.

It's human nature for our automatic pilot to kick in and for behavior and performance to become humdrum and predictable in circumstances that are common, whether at the breakfast table, the bedroom, or the office.

It could have started one morning when you overslept. Rather than spending a lot of time picking your outfit, you just threw something together . . . and no one seemed to notice the difference.

Maybe it began the day you had an idea but didn't mention it because your supervisor had nixed your last five proposals.

Whenever the seed was planted, it was nourished by the increasing sense of security you developed about your ability to get the job done and your place in the company. But as you're all too well aware, nobody is secure anymore.

Even though you've fallen into this pattern you *can* make sure your name doesn't end up on a list of employees who aren't "adding value." You *can* regain the spark you had when you first joined the company.

Appearance and Image Count

Start by spending more time in front of the mirror each morning. Obviously your grooming must be impeccable and your clothing clean and pressed. But you also have to think about the message your appearance is conveying.

Forget about making statements. Your ceramic Richard Nixon cuff links may be on the cutting edge of fashion and a hoot to boot—but they don't match your employer's image of the model employee.

It's easy to determine exactly what that image entails: just look at how your boss dresses. If he doesn't wear corduroys to work, then keep yours in the closet. If he wears only suits, do likewise. You want your supervisor to look at you and see a reflection of himself.

Don't be so obvious that the two of you end up looking like identical twins. The effect should be subliminal. To achieve that, try to replicate the essential elements of your supervisor's style— for example, solid-colored, classically cut suits with a white shirt and primary-colored tie.

If your change in attire generates any comments, just say that you've realized you're actually more comfortable dressed this way.

Look Fresh All Day Long

Check your hair (and makeup) several times during the day. After lunch spend a few moments brushing your teeth and cleansing your breath. Refrain from kicking off your shoes or removing your jacket unless the air-conditioning breaks down *and* your boss does so first.

Every time you're about to go out of your personal office or work area, make sure you look just as you did when you arrived that morning.

Look Cheerful and Enthusiastic

Don't forget to smile. If you look cheerful, your boss will perceive you as enthusiastic, happy, and loyal. You'll be seen as a positive force, someone who adds value to the company morale. Those who frown are seen as detracting from morale and, therefore, the bottom line.

Don't deceive yourself into thinking such superficial matters as your outfit and expression aren't important. If you look like a good employee, your boss will have an added reason to perceive you as a good employee. Conversely, dress slovenly and frown all the time and your boss will have a reason to perceive you as an inefficient, disruptive employee. I believe that once your boss makes a superficial judgment of you, he'll look for evidence to back it up.

Don't Get Involved in Office Gossiping

Stop gossiping and slinging mud. You can listen to what's being said—it could be valuable information—but don't participate. Live by that old adage "If you've nothing nice to say, say nothing." If pressed for an opinion, say something positive or noncommittal.

I'm not suggesting you "sell out." I believe principles are important and would never suggest compromising your ideals when it comes to freedom of speech and religion or ethnic, racial, or gender equality. I'm just counseling prudence. Which is more important, your job or wearing the Richard Nixon cuff links?

Stop Watching the Clock

Another way to better your image is to show up early and stay late. Managers and executives think those who work longer hours are more productive, and being productive equals adding value. Bosses also think time equals commitment. Your stock will rise if your boss sees you at your post before everyone else arrives and still there after everyone else heads home.

Become a Student of Your Company and Industry

Fill those extra hours in the office by becoming a student of your company and industry. Keep up with industry trends and how they affect your company. Don't worry about demonstrating your knowledge; it will come out in the normal course of business.

Find out the Company's Priorities and Make Them Your Own

Does your boss use the word "quality" in every presentation he makes? Is cost efficiency the new company motto? Come up with a way to demonstrate to your boss that you're "with the program."

Become a Human Suggestion Box

One way to show you're with the program is to offer ideas and suggestions. But before suggesting anything, consider its impact on the bottom line. Make sure your suggestions are as selfless as possible, demonstrating that your priority is the company, not yourself.

Make Your Value to the Company Clear

Every company values employees who are personally responsible for making the company money, saving the company money, or saving the company time. You can make sure your boss is aware of your contribution by having some third party bring it to her attention. For instance, if a client compliments you, ask him to pass the message on to your boss.

If You're Not Adding Value, Start

If you're not adding value to your company, start . . . immediately. Make your department more productive or efficient. Cultivate some loyal customers. Become an expert in something important to the company's future. Fill vacuums in the company.

Add to Your Bundle of Skills

Managers today are looking for well-rounded employees able to take on many different tasks and roles. Therefore the more skills you have, the more valuable you'll be. If your company offers training programs, take advantage of them. Pursue outside academic and technical study. In order to let your boss know you're adding to your skills, ask his advice about a particular course or program. Even if he can't help you, you'll have sent the right message.

Begin a Dialogue with Your Boss

Consider scheduling a one-on-one meeting with your boss in order to reinforce all your previous efforts. Simply express your love of the company and your eagerness to make sure you're on the right track. If you've done everything else well, seeking and getting reassurance from your boss should guarantee your safety for at least another six months. Even if you learn you're not on the right course, you'll have heard about it early enough to either take corrective steps or begin the starting over process once again.

The New Rules of the Workplace

Now that you've cleaned up your act on the job, it's important for you to accept that there are new rules in the workplace, even though you haven't changed companies or jobs.

- Security is now a function of skill, not of seniority or experience.
- Security comes from things you create—networks, reputation, initiatives—not from things the company gives you.
- Security comes from making a unique contribution, not from following orders.

197

- Security comes from a sense of self-confidence and self-sufficiency, not from dependence on your boss.
- Everyone is really a contingency worker, so you have to approach your work as if you were an independent contractor or freelancer rather than an employee.
- Think of yourself as being self-employed even though you're not. That means accepting ultimate responsibility for your own health insurance, retirement pension, training, and skill improvement.
- Realize that from now on job benefits will come from the nature of the work you're doing, not from things added to your compensation. Chances for education and training will take the place of company cars and expense accounts.
- You must constantly demonstrate your value to the organization as a flexible, knowledgeable, multiskilled team player.
- You must never fall in love with a company . . . because it's never going to love you back.

For More Information

For more sources of information on how to succeed in today's workplace, see Appendix Five on page 231.

APPENDIX ONE

Resources for Job Hunters

For more information about the changes taking place in the job market and the American economy, take a look at the following books:

- *Age of Unreason* by Charles Handy (Harvard Business School Press, 1991)
- *Career Crash: The End of America's Love Affair with Work* by Barry Glassner (Simon & Schuster, 1994)
- *Declining Fortunes: The Withering of the American Dream* by Katherine S. Newman (Basic Books, 1994)
- *End of Work: The Decline of the Global Labor Force and the Dawn of the Post Market Era* by Jeremy Rifkin (Putnam, 1994)
- *Job Shift: How to Prosper in a Workplace without Jobs* by William Bridges (Addison-Wesley, 1994)
- *Jobless Future: Sci-Tech and the Dogma of Work* by Stanley Aronowitz and William DiFazio (University of Minnesota Press, 1994)
- *We Are All Self-Employed: A New Social Contract Affecting Every Worker and Organization* by Cliff Hakim (Berrett-Koehler, 1994)

For more information on traditional job hunting, consider these books:

- *Conquer Résumé Objections* by Robert F. Wilson and Erik H. Rambusch (Wiley, 1994)
- *Executive Job-Changing Workbook* by John Lucht (Holt, 1994)
- *How to Win the Job You Really Want* by Janice Weinberg (Holt, 1995)
- *It's Who You Know: Career Strategies for Making Effective Personal Contacts* by Cynthia Chin-Lee (Pfeiffer, 1993)
- *Knock 'em Dead: With Great Answers to Tough Interview Questions* by Martin Yate (Bob Adams, 1992)
- *Mastering the Hidden Job Market: How to Create New Job Opportunities in a World of Uncertainty and Change* by Tom Jackson (Random House, 1992)
- *Networking* by Douglas B. Richardson (Wiley, 1994)
- *Overnight Job Change Letters* by Donald Asher (Ten Speed Press, 1994)
- *Staying in Demand: How to Make Job Offers Come to You* by Carl D. Peterson (McGraw-Hill, 1993)
- *Suddenly Unemployed: How to Survive Unemployment and Land a Better Job!* by Helen Hosier (Nelson, 1992)
- *Winning Image: Present Yourself with Confidence and Style for Career Success* by James Gray (AMACOM, 1993)

For more information on economic, demographic, and social trends in American society, look at these sources:

- *American Demographics* magazine, available at good newsstands and most libraries
- Census Bureau (http://www.census.gov), all the numbers you could possibly want or need, directly from the source
- FINWeb (http://www.finweb.com), economic information and links to economic journals, databases, and working papers, maintained by the University of Texas at Austin
- *Generations: The History of America's Future, 1584 to 2069* by William Strauss and Neil Howe (William Morrow, 1991)

- *Great Expectations: America and the Baby Boom Generation* by Landon Jones (Ballantine, 1981)
- Net Economics Project (http://netec.wustl.edu/netec.html), a searchable database of economic working papers from more than 200 universities, maintained by Washington University in St. Louis
- *The Master Trend: How the Baby Boom Generation Is Remaking America* by Cheryl Russell (Plenum, 1993)
- *The Popcorn Report* by Faith Popcorn (Doubleday, 1991)

For more information on changing careers, consider the following books:

- *Career-Shifting: Starting Over in a Changing Economy* by William Charland (Bob Adams, 1993)
- *It's Never Too Late: One Hundred Fifty Men and Women Who Changed Their Careers* by Robert K. Otterbourg (Barron, 1993)
- *Kiplinger's Survive and Profit from a Mid-Career Change* by Dan Moreau (Kiplinger Books, 1994)
- *Second Careers: New Ways to Work after Fifty* by Caroline Bird (Little Brown, 1992)

For information on specific companies and industries, consider these Web pages on the Internet:

- CommerceNet (http://www.comerce.net): an index of the Web pages of major companies and businesses providing annual reports, quarterly earnings, and promotional and product literature
- Dun & Bradstreet (http://www.dbisna.com): a database of corporate profiles and financial reports on privately held companies—a background report on a company costs $20
- EINet Galaxy's Business and Commerce Directory (htt://galaxy.einet.net/galaxy/Business-and-Commerce.html): a linked directory of alphabetically arranged business topics
- Hoover's Online (http://www.hoovers.com): information on

approximately 10,000 companies, including job announce-
ments
- Securities and Exchange Commission (http://www.sec.gov):
mandatory on-line SEC filings from 1994 to today
- World Wide Web Virtual Library's Catalog of Electronic
Journals (http://www.edoc.com/ejournal): a directory of the
consumer, trade, and professional journals, newsletters, and
magazines that can be found in electronic form on the Internet

Here are some books intended to help you discover the "perfect job" for you. They can be excellent aides for self-assessment
and self-discovery:

- *Career Anchors: Discovering Your Real Values* by Edgar H. Schein
(Pfeiffer, 1993)
- *Childhood Dreams—Career Answers: A Woman's Practical and
Playful Guide to the Career Puzzle* by Marti Chaney and Vicki
Thayer (Lifeworks Press, 1992)
- *Do What You Are: Discover the Perfect Career for You through the
Secrets of Personality Type* by Paul D. Tieger and Barbara Barron-
Tieger (Little Brown, 1992)
- *Finding the Hat That Fits: How to Turn Your Heart's Desire into Your
Life's Work* by John Caple (Nal-Dutton, 1993)
- *I Could Do Anything If I Only Knew What It Was: How to Discover
What You Really Want and How to Get It* by Barbara Sher and
Barbara Smith (Delacorte, 1994)
- *Stop Postponing the Rest of Your Life* by Paul Stevens (Ten-Speed
Press, 1993)
- *What Color Is Your Parachute 1994* by Richard Bolles (Ten-
Speed Press, 1993)
- *Wishcraft: How to Get What You Really Want* by Barbara Sher and
Anne Gottlieb (Ballantine, 1986)
- *Work with Passion: How to Do What You Love for a Living* by
Nancy Anderson (Carrol & Graf, 1984)

APPENDIX TWO

Resources for Entrepreneurs

The shelves of bookstores and libraries are overflowing with excellent general books on how to start and manage small businesses. I've tried to focus this list on books that deal either with one aspect of starting a business or with starting a particular type of business. I'm sure I've left off some good ones, so use this as a starting point rather than a comprehensive guide.

- *Accounting for the New Business: How to Do Your Own Accounting Simply, Easily, and Accurately* by Christopher Malburg (Bob Adams, 1994)
- *Advertising Handbook: Make a Big Impact with a Small Business Budget* by Dell Dennison and Linda Tobey (Self-Counsel Press, 1991)
- *All in One Business Planning Guide: How to Create Cohesive Plans for Marketing, Sales, Operations, Finance, and Cash Flow* by Christopher Malburg (Bob Adams, 1994)
- *Anatomy of a Business Plan* by Linda Pinson and Jerry Jinnett (Dearborn Financial, 1993)
- *Be the Boss II: Running a Successful Service Business* by Sandi Wilson (Avon, 1993)

- *BioBusiness Handbook: How to Organize and Operate a Biotechnology Business* by Michael G. Pappas (Humana, 1994)
- *Bottom-Line Basics: Understand and Control Business Finances* by Robert J. Low (Oasis Press, 1994)
- *Building an Import/Export Business* by Kenneth D. Weiss (Wiley, 1991)
- *Business Plans That Win: Lessons from the MIT Enterprise Forum* by Stanley Rich and David Grumpert (HarperCollins, 1987)
- *Catering: Start and Running a Money-Making Business* by Judy Richards (McGraw-Hill, 1994)
- *Collection Techniques for a Small Business* by Gini Graham Scott and John J. Harrison (Oasis Press, 1994)
- *Complete Book of Small Business Legal Forms* by Daniel Sitarz (Nova, 1991)
- *Consignment Boutique Primer: Entrepreneurship for the Lady Who Loves Apparel and People* by Nimi Wanek and Ken Meyer (Meyer–Man Books, 1992)
- *Crafting the Successful Business Plan* by Erik Hyypia (Prentice-Hall, 1992)
- *Drywall Contractor: Start and Run a Money-Making Business* by Anthony Dougherty (TAB Books, 1995)
- *Ecopreneuring: The Complete Guide to Small Business Opportunities from the Environmental Revolution* by Steven J. Bennett (Wiley, 1991)
- *Electrical Contractor: Start and Run a Money-Making Business* by Dan Ramsey (McGraw-Hill, 1993)
- *Entrepreneurial PC: The Complete Guide to Starting a PC-Based Business* by Bernard J. David (McGraw-Hill, 1994)
- *Ernst and Young Business Plan Guide* by Eric S. Siegel, Brian R. Ford, and Jay M. Burnstein (Wiley, 1993)
- *Finding Money for Your Small Business: The One-Stop Guide to Raising All the Money You Will Need* by Max Fallek (Dearborn Financial, 1994)
- *From Dogs to Riches: A Step-by-Step Guide to Start and Operate Your Own Mobile Cart Vending Business. Includes Merchandise and Food Carts* by Vera D. Clark–Rugley (MCC Publishing, 1993)

- *Getting Paid in Full: Collect the Money You Are Owed and Develop a Successful Credit Policy* by Kelsea W. Wilbur (Sourcebooks, 1993)
- *Growing Your Home-Based Business: A Complete Guide to Proven Sales and Marketing Communications Strategies* by Kim T. Gordon (Prentice-Hall, 1992)
- *Guerrilla Advertising: Cost-Effective Tactics for Small Business Success* by Jay C. Levinson (Houghton Mifflin, 1984)
- *Guerrilla Financing: Alternative Techniques to Finance Any Small Business* by Bruce Blechman and Jay C. Levinson (Houghton Mifflin, 1992)
- *Guerrilla Marketing Attack: New Strategies, Tactics, and Weapons for Winning Big Profits* by Jay C. Levinson (Houghton Mifflin, 1989)
- *Guerrilla Selling: Unconventional Tactics for Increasing Your Sales* by Bill Gallagher (Houghton Mifflin, 1992)
- *Hire the Best . . . and Avoid the Rest* by Michael W. Mercer (AMACOM, 1993)
- *Home Business Desk Reference: Everything You Need to Know to Start and Run Your Home-Based Business* by David R. Eyler (Wiley, 1994)
- *How to Be Successful in the Antique Business: A Survival Handbook* by Ronald S. Barlow (Windmill Publishing, 1980)
- *How to Develop the Restaurant Business: Promotion of the Chinese Restaurant Take-Out Order Business* by Chau Liang (Gold Town Sales, 1993)
- *How to Make Twenty Thousand Dollars a Year in Antiques* by Bruce E. Johnson (Ballantine, 1987)
- *How to Manage a Successful Bar* by Christopher Egerton-Thomas (Wiley, 1994)
- *How to Open and Run a Successful Restaurant* by Christopher Egerton-Thomas (Wiley, 1995)
- *How to Open Your Own Store* by Mike Antoniak (Avon, 1994)
- *How to Own and Operate a Card and Gift Shop* by Patti Brickman (Greeting Card Association, 1988)
- *How to Promote, Publicize, and Advertise Your Growing Business:*

Getting the Word Out Without Spending a Fortune by Kim Baker and Sunny Baker (Wiley, 1992)
- *How to Start a Business without Quitting Your Job: The Moonlight Entrepreneur's Guide* by Philip Holland (Ten-Speed Press, 1992)
- *How to Start a Home-Based Business* by Mike Antoniak (Avon, 1995)
- *How to Start a Mail-Order Business (for under $10,000)* by Mike Powers (Avon, 1996)
- *How to Start a Retirement Business* by Jacquie Powers (Avon, 1996)
- *How to Start a Service Business* by Ben Chant and Melissa Morgan (Avon, 1994)
- *How to Start a Window Cleaning Business: A Guide to Sales, Procedures and Operations* by Judy Suvall (Cleaning Consultants, 1988)
- *How to Start a Word Processing-Secretarial Business: Be Your Own Boss and Never Fetch Coffee Again!* by Louise Hagan (Whyte Rose, 1994)
- *How to Start and Build a Successful Manufacturers' Agency* by James Gibbons (Prentice-Hall, 1988)
- *How to Start and Operate a Mail Order Business* by Julian L. Simon (McGraw-Hill, 1993)
- *How to Start and Operate a Recycling Business* by John P. Allison (RMC Publishing Group, 1991)
- *How to Start and Run a Writing and Editing Business* by Herman Holtz (Wiley, 1992)
- *How to Start and Run Your Own Retail Business* by Irving Burstiner (Carol Publishing Group, 1994)
- *How to Turn Your FAX Machine into a Money Machine* by Marcia J. Hootman (New Wave, 1993)
- *HVAC Technician: Start and Run a Money-Making Business* by R. Dodge Woodson (TAB Books, 1994)
- *Information for Sale* by John H. Everet (McGraw-Hill, 1994)
- *Is There a Product Inside You?: How to Successfully Develop and Market Any Product* by Reece A. Franklin (AAJA Publishing Company, 1990)

- *Mail-Order Riches Success Kit* by Tyler G. Hicks (International Wealth, 1994)
- *Mailing List Services on Your Home-Based PC* by Linda Rohrbough (TAB Books, 1993)
- *Marketing Magic: Innovative and Proven Ideas for Finding Customers, Making Sales, and Growing Your Business* by Don Debelak (Bob Adams, 1994)
- *Mid-Career Entrepreneur: How to Start a Business and Be Your Own Boss* by Joseph R. Mancuso (Dearborn Financial, 1993)
- *Money in Your Mailbox: How to Start and Operate a Successful Mail-Order Business* by Perry L. Wilbur (Wiley, 1992)
- *One Thousand One Hundred One Businesses You Can Start from Home* by Daryl A. Hall (Wiley, 1995)
- *One Thousand One Ideas to Create Retail Excitement* by Edgar A. Falk (Prentice-Hall, 1994)
- *Open Your Own Bed and Breakfast* by Barbara Notarius and Gail Sforza Brewer (Wiley, 1992)
- *Painting Contractor: Start and Run a Money-Making Business* by Dan Ramsey (TAB Books, 1993)
- *Personal Selling Strategies for Consultants and Professionals: The Perfect Sales Equation* by Richard K. Carlson (Wiley, 1993)
- *Professional Cleaning and Building Maintenance: How to Organize a Money-Saving Business or Department for Floor and Building Care* by Bill Clarke (Cleaning Consultants, 1965)
- *Selling What You Make: Profit from Your Handcrafts* by James E. Seitz (McGraw-Hill, 1992)
- *Start and Run a Money-Making Bar* by Bruce Fier (McGraw-Hill, 1993)
- *Start and Run a Profitable Bed and Breakfast: Your Step-by-Step Business Plan* by Monica Taylor and Richard Taylor (Self-Counsel Press, 1992)
- *Start and Run a Profitable Catering Business: From Thyme to Timing: Your Step-by-Step Business Plan* by George Erdosh (Self-Counsel Press, 1994)
- *Start and Run a Profitable Consulting Business: Your Step-by-Step Business Plan* by Douglas Gray (Self-Counsel Press, 1990)

- *Start and Run a Profitable Craft Business: Your Step-by-Step Business Plan* by William Hynes (Self-Counsel Press, 1993)
- *Start and Run a Profitable Freelance Writing Business: Your Step-by-Step Business Plan* by Christine Adamec (Self-Counsel Press, 1994)
- *Start and Run a Profitable Home-Based Business: Your Step-by-Step First Year Guide* by Edna Sheedy (Self-Counsel Press, 1990)
- *Start and Run a Profitable Home Daycare: Your Step-by-Step Business Plan* by Catherine Pruissen (Self-Counsel Press, 1993)
- *Start and Run a Profitable Restaurant: Your Step-by-Step Business Plan* by Michael M. Coltman (Self-Counsel Press, 1994)
- *Start and Run a Profitable Retail Business: Your Step-by-Step Business Plan* by Michael M. Coltman (Self-Counsel Press, 1993)
- *Start and Run a Profitable Travel Agency: Your Step-by-Step Business Plan* by Richard Cropp and Barbara Braidwood (Self-Counsel Press, 1993)
- *Start and Run Your Own Profitable Service Business* by Irving Burstiner (Prentice-Hall, 1992)
- *Start Your Own Business: After Fifty—Sixty—Or Seventy!* by Lauraine Snelling (Bristol, 1990)
- *Start Your Own Coffee and Tea Store* (Pfeiffer & Company, 1994)
- *Start Your Own Construction and Land Development Business* by Adam Starchild (Nelson-Hall, 1983)
- *Start Your Own Desktop Publishing Business* (Pfeiffer & Company, 1994)
- *Start Your Own Gift Basket Business* (Pfeiffer & Company, 1994)
- *Start Your Own Import-Export Business* (Pfeiffer & Company, 1994)
- *Start Your Own Mail-Order Business* (Pfeiffer & Company, 1994)
- *Start Your Own Money-Making Computer Business* (Pfeiffer & Company, 1994)
- *Start Your Own Résumé Writing Business* (Pfeiffer & Company, 1994)
- *Start Your Own Secretarial Service Business* (Pfeiffer & Company, 1994)

- *Start Your Own Temporary Help Agency* by JoAnn Padgett (Pfeiffer & Company, 1994)
- *Start, Run and Profit from Your Own Home-Based Business* by Gregory F. Kishel and Patricia G. Kishel (Wiley, 1991)
- *Starting a Business in Your Home* by Tonya Bolden (Longmeadow, 1993)
- *Starting a Business to Sell Your Artwork* (Business of Your Own, 1988)
- *Starting a Business to Sell Your Craft Items* (Business of Your Own, 1988)
- *Starting a Clothing Boutique* (Business of Your Own, 1988)
- *Starting a Day Care Center* (Business of Your Own, 1988)
- *Starting a Flower Shop* (Business of Your Own, 1988)
- *Starting a Gift Shop* (Business of Your Own, 1988)
- *Starting a Home-Based Business (Full or Part-Time)* by Irene Korn and Bill Zanker (Carol Publishing Group, 1992)
- *Starting a Mail-Order Business* (Business of Your Own, 1988)
- *Starting a Public Relations Firm* (Business of Your Own, 1988)
- *Starting a Secretarial Service* (Business of Your Own, 1988)
- *Starting an Antique Shop* (Business of Your Own, 1988)
- *Starting and Building Your Own Accounting Business* by Jack Fox (Wiley, 1991)
- *Starting and Operating a Landscape Maintenance Business* by Laurence W. Price (Botany Books, 1989)
- *Starting Your Business: Tax Guide 203* by Holmes F. Crouch (Allyear Tax, 1992)
- *Stealing Home: How to Leave Your Job and Become a Successful Consultant* by Peter C. Brown (Crown Publishing Group, 1994)
- *Successful Business Plan: Secrets and Strategies* by Rhonda M. Abrams (Oasis Press, 1993)
- *The Learning Annex Guide to Starting Your Own Import-Export Business* by Karen Offitzer (Carol Publishing Group, 1992)
- *Upstart Guide to Owning and Managing a Bar or Tavern* by Roy S. Alonzo (Upstart, 1994)
- *Upstart Guide to Owning and Managing a Bed and Breakfast* by Lisa Angowski Rogak (Upstart, 1994)

- *Upstart Guide to Owning and Managing a Consulting Service* by Dan Ramsey (Upstart, 1994)
- *Upstart Guide to Owning and Managing a Desktop Publishing Business* by Dan Ramsey (Upstart, 1994)
- *Upstart Guide to Owning and Managing a Florist Service* by Dan Ramsey (Upstart, 1994)
- *Upstart Guide to Owning and Managing a Newsletter Business* by Lisa Angowski Rogak (Upstart, 1994)
- *Upstart Guide to Owning and Managing a Résumé Service* by Dan Ramsey (Upstart, 1994)
- *Upstart Guide to Owning and Managing a Travel Service* by Dan Ramsey (Upstart, 1994)
- *Upstart Guide to Owning and Managing an Antiques Business* by Lisa Angowski Rogak (Upstart, 1994)
- *Walking the High-Tech High Wire: The Technical Entrepreneur's Guide to Running a Successful Enterprise* by David Adamson (McGraw-Hill, 1993)
- *You Can Start Your Own Daycare* by Elizabeth F. Jones (Washington Publishing Company, 1990)
- *Your Home Business Can Make Dollars and Sense* by Jo Frohbieter-Mueller (Chilton, 1990)
- *Your Own Shop: How to Open and Operate a Successful Retail Business* by Ruth Jacobson (McGraw-Hill, 1991)

Here's a list of national associations and organizations that provide service and advice to small business owners. I've tried to include a sentence or two about the group's primary mission.

- Alliance for Fair Competition, 3 Bethesda Metro Center, Ste. 1100, Bethesda, MD 20814, (410) 235-7116, fax (410) 235-7116. Combats anticompetitive and unfair trade practices by utilities.
- American Association for Consumer Benefits, P.O. Box 100279, Fort Worth, TX 76185, (800) 872-8896, fax (817) 735-1726. Promotes the availability of medical and other benefits to small business owners.

- American Small Business Association, 1800 N. Kent St., Ste. 910, Arlington, VA 22209, (800) 235-3298. Supports legislation favorable to the small business enterprise.
- American Woman's Economic Development Corporation, 71 Vanderbilt Ave., 3rd fl., New York, NY 10169, (212) 692-9100, fax (212) 692-9296. Sponsors training and technical assistance programs.
- Association of Small Business Development Centers, 1313 Farnam, Ste. 132, Omaha, NE 68182, (402) 595-2387. Local centers providing advice for those planning to establish a small business.
- BEST Employers Association, 4201 Birch St., Newport Beach, CA 92660, (800) 854-7417, (714) 756-1000, fax (714) 553-0883. Provides small independent businesses with managerial, economic, financial, and sales information helpful for business improvement.
- Business Coalition for Fair Competition, 1101 King St., Alexandria, VA 22314, (703) 739-2782. Seeks to eliminate unfair advantages of tax-exempt organizations that sell and lease products and services in the commercial marketplace.
- Business Market Association, 4131 N. Central Expy., Ste. 720, Dallas, TX 75204, (214) 559-3900, fax (214) 559-4143. Works to bring large corporate lobbying and benefits to companies who do not have the workforce to achieve those benefits.
- Coalition of Americans to Save the Economy, 1100 Connecticut Ave, NW, Ste. 1200, Washington, D.C. 20036, (800) 752-4111. Works to protect the rights of small businesses by opposing the practice of national discount store chains demanding that suppliers discontinue the use of independent manufacturer's representatives.
- Home Executives National Networking Association, P.O. Box 6223, Bloomingdale, IL 60108, (708) 307-7130. Aims to provide opportunities for personal and professional growth to home-based business owners.
- Independent Small Business Employers of America, 520 S. Pierce, Ste. 224, Mason City, IA 50401, (515) 424-3187, (800)

728-3187. Works to assist members in keeping their businesses profitable by maintaining good employee relations.

- International Association for Business Organizations, P.O. Box 30149, Baltimore, MD 21270, (410) 581-1373. Establishes international business training institutions.
- International Council for Small Business, c/o Jefferson Smurfit Center for Entrepreneurial Studies, St. Louis University, 3674 Lindell Blvd., St. Louis, MO 63108, (314) 658-3896, fax (314) 658-3897. Fosters discussion of topics pertaining to small business management.
- International Association of Business, 701 Highlander Blvd., Arlington, TX 76015, (817) 465-2922, fax (817) 467-5920. Keeps members informed of trends in the business industry.
- Mothers' Home Business Network, P.O. Box 423, East Meadow, NY 11554, (516) 997-7394. Offers advice and support services on how to begin a successful business at home; helps members communicate with others who have chosen the same career option.
- Nation of Ishmael, 2696 Ben Hill Rd., East Point, GA 30344, (404) 349-1153. Nondenominational religious organization working to improve the economic, educational, spiritual, and social potential of black communities in the United States.
- National Association for Business Organizations, P.O. Box 30149, Baltimore, MD 21270, (410) 581-1373. Represents the interests of small businesses to government and community organizations on small business affairs.
- National Association for the Cottage Industry, P.O. Box 14850, Chicago, IL 60614, (312) 472-8116. Acts as an advocacy group for cottage workers.
- National Association for the Self-Employed, P.O. Box 612067, Dallas, TX 75261-2067, (800) 551-4446. Acts as a forum for the exchange of ideas.
- National Association of Home-Based Businesses, P.O. Box 30220, Baltimore, MD 21270, (410) 363-3698. Provides support and development services to home-based businesses.
- National Association of Private Enterprise, P.O. Box 612147,

Dallas TX 75261-2147, (817) 428-4236, (800) 223-6273, fax (817) 332-4525. Seeks to ensure the continued growth of private enterprise through education, benefits programs, and legislation.

- National Business Association, 5025 Arapaho, Ste. 515, Dallas, TX 75248, (214) 991-5381, (800) 456-0440, fax (214) 960-9149. Promotes and assists the growth and development of small businesses.
- National Business Owners Association, 1200 18th St. NW, Ste. 500, Washington, D.C. 20036, (202) 737-6501, fax (202) 737-3909. Promotes the interests of small business.
- National Federation of Independent Business, 53 Century Blvd., Ste. 300, Nashville, TN 37214, (615) 872-5800. Presents opinions of small and independent business to state and national legislative bodies.
- National Small Business Benefits Association, 2244 N. Grand Ave. E., Springfield, IL 62702, (217) 753-2558, fax (217) 753-2558. Offers discounts on group dental and life insurance, nationwide paging and travel programs, car rental, fax equipment, office supplies, and cellular phone services.
- National Small Business United, 1155 15th St. NW, Ste. 710, Washington, D.C. 20005, (202) 293-8830, (800) 345-6728, fax (202) 872-8543. Purposes are to promote free enterprise and to foster the birth and vigorous development of independent small businesses.
- Service Corps of Retired Executives Association, 409 3rd St. SW, Ste. 5900, Washington, D.C. 20024, (202) 205-6762, fax (202) 205-7636. Volunteer program sponsored by U.S. Small Business Administration in which active and retired businessmen and businesswomen provide free management assistance to men and women who are considering starting a small business, encountering problems with their business, or expanding their business.
- Small Business Assistance Center, 554 Main St., P.O. Box 1441, Worcester, MA 01601, (508) 756-3513, fax (508) 791-4709. Offers planning and strategy programs to aid busi-

nesspersons in starting, improving, or expanding small businesses.

- Small Business Exporters Association, 4603 John Tyler Ct., Ste. 203, Annandale, VA 22003, (703) 642-2490, fax (703) 750-9655. Promotes interests of small export companies.
- Small Business Foundation of America, 1155 15th St., Washington, D.C. 20005, (202) 223-1103, fax (202) 872-8543. Charitable organization that raises funds for educational and research on small businesses.
- Small Business Legislative Council, 1156 15th St. NW, Ste. 510, Washington, D.C. 20005, (202) 639-8500. Permanent independent coalition of trade and professional associations that share a common commitment to the future of small business.
- Small Business Network, P.O. Box 30149, Baltimore, MD 21270, (410) 581-1373. Provides management and marketing services, business evaluations, and import and export management services.
- Small Business Service Bureau, 554 Main St., P.O. Box 1441, Worcester, MA 01601-1441, (508) 756-3513, fax (508) 791-4709. Provides national assistance concerning small business group insurance, cash flow, taxes, and management problems.
- Support Services Alliance, P.O. Box 130, Schohaire, NY 12157-0130, (518) 295-7966, (800) 322-3920, fax (518) 295-8556. Provides services and programs such as group purchasing discounts, health coverage, legislative advocacy, and business and financial support services.

Here's a list of regional organizations that can provide information, advice, and guidance for your entrepreneurial efforts:

- Alabama Small Business Development Center Consortium, University of Alabama at Birmingham, Medical Towers Bldg. 1, Birmingham, AL 35294, (205) 934-7260
- Alaska Small Business Development Center, University of Alaska Anchorage, 430 W. 7th Ave., Ste. 110, Anchorage, AK 99501, (907) 274-7232

- Arkansas Small Business Development Center, University of Arkansas at Little Rock, 100 S. Main, Ste. 410, Little Rock, AR 72201, (501) 324-9043
- SCORE Chapter 503, 1700 E. Florida Ave., Hemet, CA 92344, (909) 652-4390
- California Small Business Development Center Program, Department of Commerce, 801 K St., Ste. 1700, Sacramento, CA 95814, (916) 324-5068
- Colorado Small Business Development Center, Colorado Office of Business Development, 1625 Broadway, Ste. 1710, Denver, CO 80202, (303) 892-3809
- Connecticut Small Business Development Center, University of Connecticut, 368 Fairfield Rd., U-41, Rm. 422, Storrs, CT 06269-2041, (203) 486-4135
- Delaware Small Business Development Center, University of Delaware, Purnell Hall, Ste. 5, Newark, DE 19716-2711, (302) 831-2747
- Florida Small Business Development Association, P.O. Box 8871, Jacksonville, FL 32239, (904) 725-3980
- Florida Small Business Development Center Network, University of W Florida, Bldg. 75, Rm. 231, Pensacola, FL 32514, (904) 474-3016
- Georgia Small Business Development Center, University of Georgia, Chicopee Complex, 1180 E. Broad St., Athens, Ga 30602-5412, (706) 542-5760
- Hawaii Small Business Development Center Network, University of Hawaii at Hilo, 523 W. Lanikaula St., Hilo, HI 96720, (808) 933-3515
- Idaho Small Business Development Center, Boise State University, 1910 University Dr., Boise, ID 83725, (208) 385-1640
- Illinois Small Business Development Center, Development of Commerce and Community Affairs, 620 E. Adams St., 6th fl., Springfield, IL 62701, (217) 524-5856
- Indiana Small Business Development Center, Economic Development Council, 1 N. Capitol, Ste. 420, Indianapolis, IN 46204, (317) 264-6871

- Kokomo Small Business Development Center, 106 N. Washington, Kokomo, IN 46901, (317) 457-5301
- SCORE Chapter 50, Federal Bldg., 0130, Ft. Wayne, IN 46802
- SCORE Chapter 266, 300 N. Michigan St., South Bend, IN 46601-1239, (219) 282-4350
- SCORE Chapter 268, 100 NW 2nd St., Old Post Office, Ste. 300, Evansville, IN 47708-1202, (812) 421-5879
- Iowa Small Business Development Center, Iowa State University, 137 Lynn Ave., Ames, IA 50010, (515) 292-6351
- Kansas Small Business Development Center, Wichita State University, 1845 Fairmount, Wichita, KS 67260-0148, (316) 689-3193
- Kentucky Small Business Development Center, Center for Business Development, College of Business and Economics, Lexington, KY 40506-0034, (606) 257-7668
- SCORE Chapter 75, 800 Federal Pl., Rm. 115, Louisville, KY 40201, (502) 582-5976
- SCORE Chapter 128, 501 Broadway, Rm. B-36, Paducah, KY 42001, (502) 442-5685
- SCORE Chapter 276, 1460 Newton Pike, Lexington, KY 40511-1231
- Louisiana Small Business Development Center, Northeast Louisiana University College of Business Administration, 700 University Ave., Monroe, LA 71209-6435, (318) 342-5506
- Maryland Small Business Development Center, Dept. of Economic & Employment Development, 217 E. Redwood St., 10th fl., Baltimore, MD 21202, (410) 333-6995
- SCORE Chapter 34, c/o Federal Information Center, P.O. Box 600, Cumberland, MD 21501-0600
- Massachusetts Small Business Development Center, University of Massachusetts-Amherst, School of Management, Rm. 205, Amherst, MA 01003, (413) 545-6301
- Smaller Business Association of New England, 204 2nd Ave., P.O. Box 9117, Waltham, MA 02254-9117, (617) 890-9070
- Michigan Association of Small Businessmen, 394 W. North St., Ionia, MI 48846, (616) 527-0281

216

- Michigan Small Business Development Center, 2727 2nd Ave., Detroit, MI 48201, (313) 577-4848
- SCORE Chapter 176, 2581 I-75 Business Spur, Sault Ste. Marie, MI 49783, (906) 632-3301
- Small Business Association of Michigan, P.O. Box 16158, Lansing, MI 48901, (517) 482-8788
- Minnesota Small Business Development Center, 500 Metro Sq., 121 7th Pl., St. Paul, MN 55101-2146, (612) 297-5770
- SCORE Rochester Chapter, 220 S. Broadway, Ste. 100, Rochester, MN 55904, (507) 288-1122
- Mississippi Small Business Development Center, University of Mississippi, Old Chemistry Bldg., Ste. 216, University, MS 38677, (601) 232-5001
- Missouri Small Business Development Center, University of Missouri, 300 University Pl., Columbia, MO 65211, (314) 882-0344
- Montana Small Business Development Center, Montana Department of Commerce, 1424 9th Ave., Helena, MT 59620, (406) 444-4780
- Nebraska Small Business Development Center, University of Nebraska at Omaha, 60th and Dodge Sts., CBA Rm. 407, Omaha, NE 68182, (402) 554-2521
- Nevada Small Business Development Center, University of Nevada—Reno, College of Business Administration—032, Rm. 411, Reno, NV 89557-0100, (702) 784-1717
- New Hampshire Small Business Development Center, University of New Hampshire, 108 McConnell Hall, Durham, NH 03824, (603) 862-2200
- New Jersey Small Business Development Center, Rutgers University Graduate School of Management, 180 University Ave., Newark, NJ 07102, (201) 648-5950
- New Mexico Small Business Development Center, Santa Fe Community College, P.O. Box 4187, Santa Fe, NM 87502-4187, (505) 438-1362
- New York State Small Business Development Center, State University of New York, SUNY Central Pl., S-523, Albany, NY 12246, (518) 443-5398

- National Federation of Independent Business, North Carolina Chapter, 225 Hillsborough St., Ste. 250, P.O. Box 710, Raleigh, NC 27602-0710, (919) 755-1166
- North Carolina Small Business Development Center, University of North Carolina, 4509 Creedmoor Rd., Ste. 201, Raleigh, NC 27612, (919) 571-4154
- North Dakota Small Business Development Center, University of North Dakota, 118 Gamble Hall, UND, Box 7308, Grand Forks, ND 58202, (701) 777-3700
- Ohio Small Business Development Center, 77 S. High St., P.O. Box 1001, Columbus, OH 43226, (614) 466-2711
- SCORE Chapter 107, 200 W. 2nd St., Rm. 505, Dayton, OH 45402-1430, (513) 225-2887
- SCORE Chapter 383, Marietta College, Thomas Hall, Marietta, OH 45750, (614) 373-0260
- Oklahoma Small Business Development Center, Southeastern Oklahoma State University, P.O. Box 2584, Sta. A, Durant, OK 74701, (405) 924-0277
- Oregon Small Business Development Center, Lane Community College, 99 W. 10th Ave., Ste. 216, Eugene, OR 97401, (503) 726-2250
- Pennsylvania Small Business Development Center, the Wharton School, University of Pennsylvania, 444 Vance Hall, 3733 Spruce St., Philadelphia, PA 19104-6374, (215) 898-1219
- Puerto Rico Small Business Development Center, University of Puerto Rico, P.O. Box 5253 College Sta., Mayaguez, PR 00681, (809) 834-3590
- Rhode Island Small Business Development Center, Bryant College, 1150 Douglas Pike, Smithfield, RI 02917, (401) 232-6111
- South Carolina Small Business Development Center, University of South Carolina, 1710 College St., Columbia, SC 29208, (803) 777-4907
- South Dakota Small Business Development Center, University of South Dakota, 414 E. Clark, Vermillion, SD 57069, (605) 677-5272

- SCORE Chapter 68, Federal Bldg., Rm. 148, 167 N. Main St., Memphis, TN 38103-1816, (901) 544-3588
- Tennessee Small Business Development Center, Memphis State University, Bldg. 1, S. Campus, Memphis, TN 38152, (901) 678-2500
- North Texas—Dallas Small Business Development Center, Bill J. Priest Institute for Economic Development, 1402 Corinth St., Dallas, TX 75215, (214) 565-5833
- Northwest Texas Small Business Development Center, at Texas Tech. University, 2579 S. Loop 289, Ste. 114, Lubbock, TX 79423, (806) 745-3973
- University of Houston Small Business Development Center, University of Houston, 601 Jefferson, Ste. 2330, Houston, TX 77002, (713) 752-8444
- UTSA South Texas Border Small Business Development Center, UTSA Downtown Center, 801 S. Bowie St., San Antonio, TX 78205, (210) 224-0791
- Utah Small Business Development Center, 102 W. 500 S. Ste. 315, Salt Lake City, UT 84101, (801) 581-7905
- National Federation of Independent Business/Vermont, RR 1, Box 3517, Montpelier, VT 05602, (802) 229-9478
- Vermont Small Business Development Center, Vermont Technical College, P.O. Box 422, Randolph, VT 05060, (802) 728-9101
- Virgin Islands Small Business Development Center, University of the Virgin Islands, P.O. Box 1087, St. Thomas, VI 00804, (809) 776-3206
- Virginia Small Business Development Center, 1021 E. Cary St., 11th fl., Richmond, VA 23219, (804) 371-8253
- Washington Small Business Development Center, Washington State University, 245 Todd Hall, Pullman, WA 99164-4727, (509) 335-1576
- District of Columbia Small Business Development Center, Howard University, 6th & Fairmont Sts. NW, Rm. 128, Washington, D.C. 20059, (202) 806-1550

- SCORE Chapter 377, 1012 Main St., Wheeling, WV 26003-2785
- SCORE Chapter 488, 522 9th St., Huntington, WV 25701-2007
- West Virginia Small Business Development Center, 1115 Virginia St. E, Charleston, WV 25301, (304) 558-2960
- Wisconsin Small Business Development Center, University of Wisconsin, 432 N. Lake St., Rm. 423, Madison, WI 53706, (608) 263-7794
- Wyoming Small Business Development Center/State Network Office, 951 N. Poplar, Casper, WY 82601, (307) 235-4825

For further information on buying an existing business, take a look at the following books (I've included books on selling businesses as well since in this case it helps to understand the motivations and techniques of the other side as well):

- *Buying a Business: A Step-by-Step Guide to Purchasing a Business* by Ronald J. McGregor (MI Management Group, 1990)
- *Buying and Selling a Business: A Step-by-Step Guide* by Robert Klueger (Wiley, 1988)
- *Complete Guide to Buying a Business* by Richard W. Snowden (AMACOM, 1993)
- *Complete Guide to Selling a Business* by Michael K. Semanik and John H. Wade (AMACOM, 1994)
- *How to Buy a Business* by Richard A. Joseph, Anna M. Nekoranec, and Carl H. Steffans (Dearborn Financial, 1992)
- *Small Business Valuation Book: Easy-to-Use Techniques for Determining Fair Price, Resolving Disputes, and Minimizing Taxes* by Lawrence W. Tuller (Bob Adams, 1994)
- *Valuing a Business: The Analysis and Appraisal of Closely Held Companies* by Shannon P. Pratt, Robert F. Reilly, and Robert P. Schweibs (Irwin, 1994)
- *Valuing Small Businesses and Professional Practices* by Shannon P. Pratt, Robert F. Reilly, and Robert P. Schweibs (Irwin, 1993)

220

APPENDIX TWO

For further information on franchising, contact the following associations and take a look at the following books:

- American Association of Franchisees and Dealers (AAFD), P.O. Box 81887, San Diego, CA 92138, (800) 733-9858. Provides information and support to franchisees in their relations with franchisors.
- *Fifty Best Low-Investment, High-Profit Franchises* by Robert L. Perry (Prentice-Hall, 1994).
- *Financing Your Franchise* by Meg Whittemore, Andrew Sherman, and Ripley Hotch (McGraw-Hill, 1993).
- *Franchise Annual,* c/o Info Franchise News, 728 Center St., Box 550, Lewiston, NY 14092, (716) 754-4669. The most complete listing of the franchises available in the United States, Canada, and around the world.
- *Franchise Bible: How to Buy a Franchise or Franchise Your Own Business* by Erwin J. Kemp (Oasis Press, 1994).
- *Franchise Fraud: How to Protect Yourself Before and After You Invest* by Robert Purvin (Wiley, 1994).
- Franchise Solutions, P.O. Box 5178, Portsmouth, NH 03802, (603) 427-0569. Offers prospective franchise owners an information package, including a skill and personality assessment, information on individual franchisors, review of offering circulars, and personal consulting.
- *Franchising: The Business Concept That Changed the World* by Carrie Shook and Robert Shook (Prentice-Hall, 1993).
- *Franchising: The How to Book* by Lloyd T. Tarbutton (Prentice-Hall, 1993).
- FRANDATA, 1155 Connecticut Ave., Washington, D.C. 20036, (202) 659-8640. Publishes studies and ratings of franchisors; maintains files of Uniform Franchise Offering Circulars; information packets cost from $75 to $100 per company.
- *How to Open a Franchise Business* by Mike Powers (Avon, 1994).
- IFA Expos, c/o The Blenheim Group, 1133 Louisiana Ave., Ste.

210, Winter Park, FL 32789, (407) 740-0018. Two-day seminars and exhibitions held in six or seven different cities around the country each year.

- International Franchise Association (IFA), 1350 New York Ave., N.W., Ste. 900, Washington, D.C. 20005, (202) 628-8000. Industry association providing information and services; publishes *The Franchise Opportunities Guide* ($15 plus $6 postage and handling), which lists information on member franchisors.
- *Starting a Franchise* (Business of Your Own, 1988).
- VETFRAN, P.O. Box 3146, Waco, TX 76707, (817) 753-4555. Provides information on program of specially discounted franchising fees and financing offers to veterans seeking to buy franchises.
- Women in Franchising, Inc., 175 N. Harbor Dr., Ste. 405, Chicago, IL 60601, (800) 222-4WIF. Sponsors workshops nationwide and provides networking assistance.

The following federal and state offices can assist you if you've questions about franchise regulations or problems or suspicions about a potential franchisor:

FEDERAL
- Office of External Affairs, U.S. Small Business Administration, 409 3rd St., SW, Rm. 7177, Washington, D.C. 20416, (202) 205-6607, fax (202) 205-7064
- Bureau of Consumer Protection, Federal Trade Commission, 6th St. & Pennsylvania Ave., Washington, D.C., NW 20580, (202) 326-2968

STATE
- Commission of Corporations, Department of Corporations, 6th fl., 3700 Wilshire Blvd., Los Angeles, CA 90010, (213) 736-2741
- Business Registration Division, Department of Commerce and Consumer Affairs, 1010 Richards St., Honolulu, HI 96813, (808) 548-5317

- Franchise Division, Office of the Attorney General, 500 S. 2nd St., Springfield, IL 62707, (217) 782-4465
- Deputy Commissioner, Franchise Division, Indiana Securities Commission, Secretary of State, 302 W. Washington, Rm. E-111, Indianapolis, IN 46204, (317) 232-6681
- Office of the Attorney General, Maryland Division of Securities, 200 St. Paul Pl., 20th fl., Baltimore, MD 21202-2020, (410) 576-6360
- Consumer Protection Division, Michigan Department of Attorney General, 670 Law Bldg., Lansing, MI 48913, (517) 373-7117
- Minnesota Department of Commerce, 133 E. 7th St., St. Paul, MN 55101, (612) 296-6328
- New York Department of Law, Bureau of Investor Protection and Securities, 120 Broadway, 23rd fl., New York, NY 10271, (212) 416-8211
- Office of Securities Commission, Capitol Bldg., Bismarck, ND 58505, (701) 224-2910
- Corporation Commission, Department of Commerce, Corporations Division, Commerce Bldg., Salem, OR 97310, (503) 378-4387
- Chief Securities Examiner, Department of Business Regulation, Securities Division, Franchise Section, Ste. 232, Providence, RI 02903-4232, (401) 277-3048
- Department of Commerce and Regulation, Division of Securities, 910 E. Sioux Ave., Pierre, SD 57501-5070, (605) 773-4823
- State Corporation Commission, Division of Securities and Retail Franchising, 1220 Bank St., Richmond, VA 23219, (804) 786-7751
- Securities Division, Washington Department of Licensing, Second fl., 405 Blake Lake Blvd., S.E., Olympia, WA 98502, (206) 753-6928
- Commissioner of Securities, Franchise Investment Division, 111 W. Wilson Street, Madison, WI 53701, (608) 266-1365

Finally, there's also a great deal of business-related information available on the Internet. Here are some sites on the World Wide Web you should take a look at:

- FedWord (http://www.fedworld.gov): business, engineering, scientific, and technical information from the U.S. government.
- IndustryNET (http://www.industry.net): a business-to-business site offering listings and catalogs from manufacturers, wholesalers, and distributors that can be searched by region or product.
- Louisiana State University Library: U.S. Federal Government Agency Directory (http://www.lib.lsu.edu/gov/fedgov.html): provides links to all the branches and departments of the federal government—such as Congress, the Department of Agriculture, and the IRS—and many independent agencies—like the Export-Import Bank of the United States and NASA.
- Small Business Administration (http://www.sbaonline. sba.gov): nearly all the excellent information available from the SBA's field offices and libraries is available here, in addition to the free business-related software programs.
- smallbizNet (http://www.lowe.org): an electronic bulletin board for entrepreneurs, including a library of books and articles that can be browsed or ordered.
- Thomas (http://thomas.loc.gov): includes the complete text of all pending federal legislation, the text of the *Congressional Record,* and E-mail addresses for representatives and senators.
- University of Sydney Fisher Library Government Internet Guide (http://lib4.fisher.su.oz.au:80/Guides/Government/index.html): a directory of Web pages for governments around the world—helpful for those doing business overseas.
- Yahoo! Business Directory (http://www.yahoo.com/business): as close to a comprehensive directory as you could find to all the business information and organization sites on the Web.
- Yahoo!'s Small Business Information (http://www.yahoo.

com/Business–and–Economy/Small–Business–Information):
an excellent directory to the small business-related sites on the
Web, along with conceptual links to areas such as financing and
consultants.

APPENDIX THREE

Resources for Returning Students

Hundreds of books are written on selecting colleges and paying for them. Most, however, are oriented toward traditional students. Still, the vast majority of information is just as applicable to you and your needs. Here's a selection of some of the books I've found to be most helpful for my clients:

- *Campus Pursuit* by G. Gary Ripple (Dearborn, 1995)
- *College Checkmate: Innovative Tuition Plans That Make You a Winner* by Debra L. Wexler (Dearborn, 1995)
- *College Majors & Careers: A Resource Guide for Effective Life Planning* by Paul Phifer (Garrett, 1993)
- *College Match: A Blueprint for Choosing the Best School for You* by Steven R. Antonoff, Ph.D., and Marie A. Friedmann, Ph.D. (Dearborn, 1995)
- *College Planning for Dummies* by Pat Ordovensky (IDG Books, 1995)
- *College Planning-Search Book* (American College Testing, 1994)
- *Do It Write: How to Prepare a Great College Application* by G. Gary Ripple (Dearborn, 1995)

- *Don't Miss Out: The Ambitious Student's Guide to Financial Aid* by Anna Leider and Robert Leider (Dearborn, 1995)
- *Earn and Learn: Your Guide to In-School Educational Employment Programs* by Joseph M. Re (Dearborn, 1995)
- *Financial Aid Financer: Expert Answers to College Financing Questions* by Joseph M. Re (Dearborn, 1995)
- *Loans and Grants from Uncle Sam: Am I Eligible and for How Much?* by Anna Leider (Dearborn, 1995)
- *Paying for Your Child's College Education* by Marguerite Smith (Warner Books, 1996)
- *Planning Your College Education* by William A. Rubinfeld (NTC Publishing Group, 1994)
- *SAT Savvy: Last Minute Tips and Strategies* by Marian and Sandra Martin (Dearborn, 1995)
- *The A's and B's of Academic Scholarships* by Debra L. Wexler (Dearborn, 1995)
- *Your Educational Plan: A Simple Guide to Planning Your College Career* (Energeia, 1995)

APPENDIX FOUR

Resources for Downshifters

There's a cottage industry in newsletters and books about downshifting. Here's a brief sampling to help you start your research and investigations:

- *Breaking Free from Corporate Bondage: Do What You Really Want to Do and Control Your Own Future* by Michael Dainard (Dearborn Financial, 1993)
- *Country Careers: Successful Ways to Live and Work in the Country* by Jerry Germer (Wiley, 1993)
- *Downshifting: Reinventing Success on a Slower Track* by Amy Saltzman (HarperCollins, 1992)
- *Essential Living,* $10/year subscription, Rt. #1, Box 1310, Moretown, VT 05660, (802) 244-1309
- *Financial Freedom in 8 Minutes a Day: How to Attract and Manage All the Money You'll Ever Need* by Ron Hulnick, Ph.D., and Mary Hulnick, Ph.D. (Rodale, 1994)
- *Making a Living Without a Job: Winning Ways for Creating Work That You Love* by Barbara Winter (Bantam, 1993)
- *Money and Emotional Conflicts* by Edmund Bergler, M.D. (Doubleday, 1959)

- *Money and the Meaning of Life* by Jacob Needleman (Doubleday, 1991)
- *Of Time, Work and Leisure* by Sebastian De Grazia (Vintage, 1994)
- *On Work, Race, and the Sociological Imagination* by Everett C. Hughes (University of Chicago Press, 1994)
- *Overworked American,* by Juliet B. Schor (Basic Books, 1991)
- *Reinvention of Work: A New Vision of Livelihood for Our Time* by Matthew Fox (HarperCollins, 1994)
- *Tightwad Gazette,* $12/year subscription, RR #1, Box 3570, Leeds, ME 04263, (207) 524-7962
- *What Are You Worth?* by Edward M. Hallowell, M.D., and William J. Grace, Jr. (Weidenfield & Nicholson, 1989)
- *Work of Her Own: A Woman's Guide to Success off the Career Track* by Susan W. Albert (Putnam, 1994)
- *Your Money or Your Life: Transforming Your Relationship with Money and Achieving Financial Independence* by Joe Dominguez and Vicki Robin (Viking, 1992)

APPENDIX FIVE

Resources for Employees

There are lots of good books about how to succeed in today's workplace. Here's a sampling:

- *Career Prescription: How to Stop Sabotaging Your Career and Put It on a Winning Track* by Anne B. Lovett (Prentice-Hall, 1994)
- *Career Survival: Strategic Job and Role Planning* by Edgar H. Schein (Pfeiffer, 1994)
- *Career Tool Kit: Skills for Success* by Carol Carter, Sarah L. Kravits, and Patricia S. Vaughan (Prentice-Hall, 1994)
- *Caught in the Middle: How to Survive and Thrive in Today's Management Squeeze* by Lynda C. Mcdermott (Prentice-Hall, 1994)
- *Empires of the Mind: Lessons to Lead and Succeed in a Knowledge-Based World* by Denis Waitley (Morrow, 1995)
- *Getting Ahead: Career Skills That Work for Everyone* by Richard Andersen (McGraw-Hill, 1994)
- *How to Fireproof Your Career: Survival Strategies for Volatile Times* by Anne Baber and Lynne Waymon (Berkley, 1995)
- *How Would Confucius Ask for a Raise?: One Hundred Solutions for Tough Business Problems* by Carol Orsborn (Morrow, 1994)

- *Just Promoted: How to Survive and Thrive in Your First 12 Months As a Manager* by Edward Betof and Frederic Harwood (McGraw-Hill, 1992)
- *Lifetime Career Manager: New Strategies for a New Era* by James C. Cabrera and Charles Albrecht (Bob Adams, 1995)
- *New Rules of the Game: The Four Key Experiences Managers Must Have to Thrive in the Non-Hierarchical 90s and Beyond* by James R. Emshoff and Teri E. Denlinger (Harper, 1992)
- *One Hundred and One Commonsense Rules for the Office: How to Get Along and Get Ahead* by John R. Brinkerhoff (Stackpole, 1992)
- *Peak Performance* by Sharon K. Ferrett (Irwin, 1993)
- *Portable Executive: Building Your Own Job Security—From Corporate Dependency to Self-Direction* by John A. Thompson and Catherine A. Henningsen (Simon & Schuster, 1995)
- *Stand Out!* by Andrew J. Dubrin (Prentice-Hall, 1993)
- *Street-Smart Career Guide: A Step-by-Step Guide to Your Career Development* by Laura Pedersen (Crown Publishing Group, 1993)
- *Succeeding: How to Become an Outstanding Professional: A Career Development Handbook* by Lee Harrisberger (Macmillan, 1993)
- *Winning the Networking Game: How to Enhance Your Career and Stay Ahead in Business* by Anne Boe (Wiley, 1994)
- *Your Own Worst Enemy: How to Overcome Career Self-Sabotage* by Andrew J. Dubrin (AMACOM, 1992)

INDEX

233

INDEX

Workplace
  books about success in, 231–32
  environment, 26, 27, 28, 38, 131
  new rules, 197–98
  new working situations, 57–58
  and office gossip, 194
  refocusing on current job, 191–97
  revolution in, 1–2
Worksheets:
  Mortgage Refinancing, 52
  Total Indebtedness, 51

World Wide Web, 86, 119
  site creation, 141
  sites for job-hunting, 67–68

Y

Yahoo, 142
Yankelovich Partners, 6